CARIBBEAN CHRONICLES

THE END OF CALICO JACK

EDDIE JONES

DRY BONES PUBLISHING

The End of Calico Jack
Copyright © 2019 by Eddie Jones

Jones, Eddie, 1957-
   The End of Calico Jack / by Eddie Jones.
     p. cm. — (Caribbean Chronicles ; book three)
     Summary: "When fourteen-year-old Ricky Bradshaw has an absence seizure episode, he finds himself in the middle of a Caribbean pirate adventure involving the infamous Calico Jack, Anne Bonny, and Mary Read." – Provided by publisher.
   ISBN-13: 978-1645262374

    [1. Pirates—Fiction. 2. Piracy—Fiction. 3. Humor—Fiction. 4. Fantasy and time trave.] I. Title.

All Scripture quotations, unless otherwise indicated, are taken from the Holy Bible, *New International Version*®, *NIV*®. Copyright © 1973, 1978, 1984, 2011 by Biblica, Inc.™ Used by permission. All rights reserved worldwide.

Any Internet addresses (websites, blogs, etc.) and telephone numbers in this book are offered as a resource. They are not intended in any way to be or imply an endorsement by the author, nor does the author vouch for the content of these sites and numbers for the life of this book.

This is a work of fiction (mostly). Names, characters, and incidents are all products of the author's imagination (sort of) or are used for fictional purposes. Any mentioned brand names, places, and trademarks remain the property of their respective owners, bear no association with the author or the publisher, and are used for fictional purposes only.

All rights reserved. No part of this publication may be reproduced, stored in a retrieval system, or transmitted in any form or by any means—electronic, mechanical, photocopy, recording, or any other—except for brief quotations in printed reviews, without the prior permission of the publisher.

Cover design: Elaina Lee
Interior design: atritex.com

Printed in the United States of America

Caribbean Chronicles Series

Book One
Curse of the Black Avenger

Book Two
Dead Calm, Bone Dry

Book Three
The End of Calico Jack

Dedication

This book is dedicated to Selma Lin.
Congrats! You booked a voyage to pirate land!

The End of Calico Jack is a fictional retelling of the life of Calico Jack, Ann Bonny, and Mary Read based on historical research. Some liberties have been taken in the telling of the story. (I was forced into piracy, after all, and taking things is what pirates do.)

Contents

1. Kidnapped by Jack Sparrow 1
2. The Strange Boy 5
3. The Scary-Looking Woman 11
4. I Learn the Scary-Looking Woman's Name 17
5. The Crew's Nest 21
6. A Sea Story 27
7. Rapids Development 37
8. Trapped 43
9. A Nation of Thieves 47
10. Hard Aground 53
11. Don't Rock Bay 57
12. Held for Ransom 61
13. My Great Plan 65
14. Preacher's Cave 67
15. A Not-So-Happy Pirate Birthday Party 73
16. My Great Plan for Capturing a British Warship 79
17. We Plot a Course for a Treasure Ship 85

18. NASSAU 87
19. HOBBLING DOBBIN 91
20. IS THE GOOD DOCTOR IN? 95
21. WE STEAL THE WILLIAM 99
22. THE BLACK PLAGUE 103
23. CALM BEFORE THE STORM 105
24. THE SQUALL BEFORE THE STORM 111
25. SCARY MARY'S MERRY MEN 115
26. HOBBLING DOBBIN EARNS HIS KEEP 119
27. THE STORM BEFORE THE STORM 125
28. THE MAELSTROM STORM 129
29. I WALK THE PLANK 133
30. THE PRIZE 137
31. NUESTRA SEÑORA DE RIQUEZA 141
32. THE TREASURE CAVE 145
33. CAPTAIN JONATHAN BARNETT 151
34. THE END OF CALICO JACK 157
35. TREASURE HUNT 163
36. A DEAD MAN'S CHEST 167
37. A TALE WORTH ITS WEIGHT IN GOLD 171

    THE ROUTES OF CALICO JACK 175
    AN HISTORICAL ACCOUNT OF CALICO JACK 177

Ship's Log
Coffin Cay

"Let's hope it doesn't happen again."

That's what Mom said to me less than an hour ago when we discovered that someone had moved the pirate treasure. "Let's hope it doesn't happen again."

Like most mothers, Mom is hoping I go back to being normal—or as normal as a boy in the tenth grade can be after he's been jettisoned out of middle school and ninth grade and hurled into the vast, chaotic cosmos known as high school where stars (popular kids like Becky Nance) collide with space debris (weird kids like me).

My name is Ricky Bradshaw and I have epilepsy.

I know what you're thinking. (Okay, not really. That's just something people say.) I bet you're thinking I have convulsions and spasms. My epilepsy isn't like that. I have what my doctors call "absence seizures." Until last Christmas I only *remember* having one seizure and that was while I was skateboarding. I have no memory of what happened during the seizure. All I know is I found myself on the sidewalk at a crosswalk with one foot on my board and the other on pavement. My subconscious had kicked in and was taking over, keeping me from riding into the street.

Most days I act and look like all the other kids in my classes. But when I have an "episode" I sort of zone out and don't even know I'm having one. Mom tells me when it happens I look like I'm daydreaming or staring off into space. Which means I pretty much look like the rest of my classmates at Quiet Cove High.

School can get pretty boring sometimes.

If you've never heard of absence seizures, that's okay. A lot of people haven't. My teachers are a lot of those people.

Last year Mrs. Dinwiddle wrote me up a bunch of times for not paying attention in class. Paying attention in school is a big deal. If there's one thing teachers want kids to do in school, it's pay attention. I'm pretty sure teachers get paid based on how well their students pay attention. I think I could go through all twelve grades without ever learning how to read, write, and add, but as long as I sat still and paid attention, I would graduate.

As you might imagine, Mom was not happy about my write-ups.

She demanded a meeting with my teachers and our assistant principal so she could explain my "condition." Mom brought articles on absence seizures and showed them videos on her phone of me having episodes. They all nodded and told Mom they were sorry. They promised Mom they would give me special attention. And they did, sort of. I didn't get written up anymore. But my classmates still made fun of me. Especially after I came back from Christmas break and they heard I had found pirate treasure.

See, Becky Nance is in my biology class and her mom is a PA at the hospital. Somehow Becky's mom heard my story about how I'd found pirate treasure, and IN CLEAR VIOLATION OF HIPPA LAWS, Becky's mom told Becky. Normally I'd be okay with Becky saying anything about me. I sort of like her, only not as much, now, because she blabbed to everyone in biology class that, "Roger swears he sailed with pirates and found treasure." (Becky thinks my name is Roger; that's how close we are as friends.)

My point is (I bet you were wondering if there *was* a point), after that incident last Christmas, Dad said we should go back to the island and cave and see if we could find the treasure. I'm pretty sure Dad thought that maybe we had hit the jackpot. I mean, the island is out in the middle of a large body of water all by itself and getting down to the cave from the top of the cliff required ropes and all.

So yesterday Mom and Dad and me arrived in Haiti, which, during pirate times, was called Hispaniola. Perhaps you've heard of Hispaniola. Hispaniola gets mentioned a lot in pirate movies. I'm not sure why. Maybe because it's close to Tortuga and Tortuga is definitely an island you're going to want to mention if you're making a pirate movie.

The three of us piled into this small, wooden fishing boat at 5 a.m. this morning and motored west, away from the village of Les Trois. On the nautical chart, the island is now called Isla de Ataúd, but when I was here with pirates they called it Coffin Cay.

After the motorboat captain dropped us off on the beach, we hiked up to the top of a sheer-face cliff that plunges straight into the surf. Using our new rock-climbing skills, we climbed down the ledge that marks the opening of the treasure cave.

The treasure is gone. I sort of figured it would be. It's been over three hundred years since I've been here. Dad pretended he wasn't disappointed, but I could tell he was. Mom, not so much. She mostly just wanted off the island and back to the air-conditioned room at the teeny-tiny motel we're staying in. (Besides, we did not really have what you would call a great plan for getting the treasure out of the cave if we had found it.) The cool thing is that I found a ship's log tucked in a crevice in the cave.

"You know what this means?" I said to my parents. "Means I really was right here in this cave."

It's a small, moldy, leather journal with the exact course and route and dates the *Nuestra Señora De Riqueza* sailed all those hundreds of years ago. The *Nuestra Señora De Riqueza* was the ship pirates raided and burned. So that proves the treasure was real and I really was here, at least in my mind.

"But we already knew that," Dad said.

"I think what your father is trying to say, honey, is that everything you experienced really happened."

"And if it can happen once," Dad said to me, "it could happen again. You could end up right back here in the land of pirates and buried treasure."

"Let's hope it doesn't happen again."

That's what Mom said to me less than an hour ago. "Let's hope it doesn't happen again."

So that's what I'm thinking about right now. *What if it does?*

We're back in the old wooden motorboat racing back to the village of Les Trois. Dad is napping on a bench seat and has his Nat's ball cap pulled over his eyes. All of Mom's focus is on the coast ahead that is bathed in golden sunlight. Far as she's concerned, we cannot get back to land fast enough. Boats and Mom are not what you would call a great combo.

I'm clutching Mom's handbag to my chest to keep it and the ship's log from getting wet. The ship's log is my only solid connection to the pirate treasure I found. The ship's log proves without a doubt that there actually was, at one time, a treasure in the cave: that I had actually seen it, touched it, held it. When I get home I'm going to show Becky Nance the ship's log. Maybe then she'll believe me. Maybe then she'll want to go out with me. Maybe then . . .

My gaze remains fixed on the horizon but I can't move.

Eyes water.

There's an acrid stench all around, like burning electrical wires.

I have this sudden intense feeling of déjà vu. A hot, tingly surge starts at the tip of my toes and shoots up to the top of my head. I swallow and . . .

. . . it happens again.

Sorry, Mom.

CHAPTER ONE

KIDNAPPED BY JACK SPARROW

Over my shoulder a hazy tropical sun hung low in the western sky. The sailing dory glided easily across the water in much the same way the motorboat had been doing moments earlier. I sailed alone. Within minutes I'd tacked into the harbor and tied off to a rickety dock.

I dropped the sail and secured it as best I could with a coarse rope, looped a line around a snapped-off piling, and stepped ashore. Horse-drawn wagons and oxcarts competed for space with pedestrians on the narrow, rutted road along the waterfront. In an open-air market, vendors sold raw fish, lobster and conch, overripe bananas, and squishy pineapples. The place had the unwelcomed smell of a trash dumpster.

You may be wondering why I didn't stay with the dory. The thought never occurred to me. It was like when you're dreaming: you don't really know you're dreaming. You think what you're seeing is really happening and sometimes if it's a bad dream it scares you. Like, in a dream you could be walking down a dark and narrow street on a tropical island with dangerous-looking men eyeing you suspiciously from the doorway of a drinking establishment and all of a sudden go … *WAIT, WHAT? Is that Jack Sparrow calling to me?*

That's what happened.

Jack Sparrow beckoned me into a grog shop.

Except it wasn't the real Jack Sparrow. Obviously. Disney would never allow the real Jack Sparrow to appear in my story.

"Psst, chico," Jack Sparrow said to me.

Jack Sparrow stood in the doorway of a grog shop called (what else?) *The Grog Shop*. Behind him stood other swarthy-looking sailors, all wearing cutlasses on hips and rings in lips and knives on belts.

"Cerveza?" Jack Sparrow held up an amber bottle. "Ron?"

Jack Sparrow spoke Spanish. Who knew?

I was not about to go into a bar with Jack Sparrow. Mom would find out. Mom always found out. Even if it was like, three hundred years before I was born, Mom would still know.

From the opposite side of the street another swarthy-looking person called to me. "You'll be want'n' ter think twice 'bout going in thar, mate."

I'm not sure why pirates talk the way they do in movies and this story, but sometimes I think I need a translator.

I looked in the direction of the other man's voice.

Directly opposite *The Grog Shop* was a dilapidated home-turned-into-a-drinking-place called *Willy's Knee*. Standing in the doorway was a tall, broad-shouldered man with a bushy mustache and beard. He wore long pants and black boots.

"Es urgente, chico," Jack Sparrow replied to the man in black boots.

2

"Urgent, says you," said Black Boots. "What'er you know 'bout urgent? Sea urchins, now they be sump'in you know a thing 'er two about."

Apparently I had stumbled into the middle of a bar war between competing drinking establishments. Smelly men from both drinking places rushed into the street and pressed in around me so close I couldn't move. It was like being at a baseball game when the benches clear; I was the poor fool trapped on the pitcher's mound, unable to escape.

One shoved me in the back; another ruffled my hair playfully. I tried to push my way through, but the men closed ranks. Some laughed, others called me "boy," "niñita," "Lady Godiva." (I still carried Mom's handbag with the ledger inside.)

But then a knife pressed against my ribs. That definitely got my attention.

Jack Sparrow whispered in my ear, "Run, guppy, and I'll gut you like a grouper. Savvy?" Still pressing the tip of his knife against my ribs, Jack Sparrow shoved me into an even darker and narrower alley.

That's when things got really bad.

CHAPTER TWO

THE STRANGE BOY

By things got really bad I mean Jack Sparrow took me to see this scary-looking woman who seemed to be the queen of the island. It happened like this.

Me: "Where are we going?"

Jack Sparrow: "Never you mind."

With me hugging Mom's handbag to my chest, we exited the alley and proceeded to the waterfront where sailors and dockhands loaded and unloaded carts and carriages. All the while I looked for a way to escape. The problem was I didn't know what island I was escaping from or which way to sail if I made it back to the dory.

Me: "Do we have to walk so fast?"

WHACK!

Me: "OW!"

WHACK! WHACK!

Jack Sparrow: "No complaining when walking."

At that very moment I spied three seedy-looking young boys clambering aboard my little sailing dory. One began untying dock lines; two others hoisted the sail. Before I could yell for them to stop, they cast off and sailed away.

So that was another way things got really bad.

Me: "I wasn't complaining. I was only …"

WHACK! WHACK! WHACK!

Past the wharf area we made our way up a path of crushed shells towards a large plantation home perched on a hill. Windows and front doors stood open. On the second level men, and a few women, reclined against top-porch railings. Some of the individuals on the balcony actually wore clothes.

We stopped at an iron gate. Beyond was a green lawn being clipped by servants with large scissors. Flowering plants lined a brick walkway leading up to the home.

I raised my hand.

Jack Sparrow: "You have a question?"

I nodded.

Jack Sparrow: "Well, spit it out, guppy."

Me: "What are we …"

WHACK!

Jack Sparrow: "Was a pop test, you stupid guppy. Get it? Pop test?"

While I imagined Jack Sparrow being cut into small pieces and fed to sharks, a stranger joined us at the gate. The strange boy wore a baggy white shirt over wine-colored baggy pants. Long, brown bangs hung over his eyes. He was somewhat pudgy around the middle and looked to be a few years older, even though he was clean-shaven.

"Appears to be a popular place," said the strange boy.

"Aye. Party never ends," Jack Sparrow said. "They'll play and make merry all night."

"Been here before have you?"

"Once or twice."

The strange boy said to me, "And you?"

Jack Sparrow gave me a sidelong glance. I looked down and focused on my dirty feet.

"Mute?" the strange boy asked Jack Sparrow.

"Sumpin' like that."

On the wide veranda, a large, black man wearing a maroon turban and puffy, brown trousers rose from a chair. Two curved swords were strapped across his oily, black chest, giving him the appearance of someone who could hurt me and would enjoy doing it.

"What business have you?" Turban Head said.

Jack Sparrow reached into his leather vest, pulled out a scrap of paper, and showed it to Turban Head.

"And you?" Turban Head said to me.

I chewed my lip and kept quiet. It seemed like the smart thing to do.

"He's with me," said Jack Sparrow.

"I am here for the ladies," the strange boy said.

Turban Head winked at the strange boy as if nothing else more needed to be said, lifted the latch, and stood aside.

We walked up the path of crushed shells and onto the porch, stepped over a snoring drunk sprawled in the doorway, and went inside the large home. A dozen or more men were gathered around an enormous walnut table, all shouting and cursing and drinking. The strange boy wandered off to chat with a scantily-clad woman who looked old enough to be his grandmother. Jack Sparrow, still holding me by the collar and his dirk pressed against my ribs, hauled me to the bar.

"I need a moment with your boss," Jack Sparrow said to an albino man pouring drinks.

"What have you done this time?"

"Not me." Jack Sparrow rolled his eyes in my direction. "Him."

THE END OF CALICO JACK

From the other side of the room a door banged open. A scary-looking woman with frizzy hair the color of a starless night sky stormed out of a back room. She wore a black velvet vest, black blouse, and black trousers. She hauled a scruffy seaman by his hair. "Get the devil out of here!" she said, kicking him in the seat of his pants. "And don't come back until your account be paid in full!"

The man, his cheeks red, tumbled over the snoring drunk lying in front of the front door, face-planted on the veranda, jumped up, and ran off.

"That goes for the rest of you scallywags. You want to hunt merchant ships and Spanish galleons, then you're welcome to my women and spirits. But if you tuck tail and run at the mere sight of a man-of-war, then by thunder there'll be the devil to pay."

As if noticing Jack Sparrow for the first time, she said to the albino bartender, "What is *he* doing here?"

"Says he has business with you."

"Does he, now?"

Jack Sparrow said, "Might I have a word?"

"A word? Here's a word. Pay up."

"Actually that's two—"

The scary-looking woman took a step forward, getting right in Jack Sparrow's face. "Don't test me. You know what happens to those who test me."

"I brought you this." When he said *this*, Jack Sparrow shoved me forward, almost into her.

"A boy? Not a sheep or goat?" I think she meant this as a joke.

But Jack Sparrow wasn't smiling. "He escaped from the gallows of Port Charles. There's a price on his head."

Though technically I had, during a previous episode, fled from Port Charles, there was not a price on my head. At least not that I was aware of.

"So he's a pirate. Look around. I have a room full of those. What I don't have a room full of are earners. Men who bring me gold and silver and precious stones. You owe me gold and silver and precious stones. Bring me those and we'll talk about your ledger. 'Till then, get the devil out of here!" She lifted her boot as if to kick Jack Sparrow in the seat of his pants.

He retreated across the room with his hands up.

"And don't come back until your account be paid in full!"

I'll be honest; I smiled.

"There's a price on your head?" she said to me.

I was going to say that Jack Sparrow was lying and that I'd never been in Port Charles, but then I said, "Yes, sort of. See I'm, ah … in the business of …" Quickly I glanced around the room at the dress and manner of the men loitering about. "… taking riches from merchant ships and Spanish galleons."

"Are you now?" Her gaze remained fixed on Mom's handbag, which I still hugged to my chest.

"Yes. And I am looking for a business partner."

I was *not* looking for a business partner. I was looking to get as far away from the scary-looking woman as possible.

"You have a name, boy?"

"Ricky Bradshaw."

The scary-looking woman said to the albino, "If you see trouble, shoot it." She wheeled and headed back toward her office. Without looking back she said to me, "Well don't just stand there looking stupid, guppy. Get in here."

I quickly followed—which is how I ended up in the scary-looking woman's office making the worst deal of the 18th century.

CHAPTER THREE

THE SCARY-LOOKING WOMAN

In the scary-looking woman's office sat a large stack of ledgers on one corner of her wooden desk: ledgers that looked almost identical to the one Mom found in the cave on Coffin Cay.

"What's in the bag?" asked the scary-looking woman.

"Presents," I said. I'm not saying my response was genius. I'm saying this was the best I could come up with while sitting across from someone who looked like she wanted to cut out my eyeballs and feed them to seagulls.

"There had better be a present in there for me."

I peeked inside Mom's handbag, praying her makeup kit was in there.

It was not.

But there was a tube of lipstick.

The scary-looking woman took it from me before I could explain how to twist and turn the tube. Which is why, seconds later, the scary-looking woman had the lips of a clown.

"State your business," the scary-looking woman said.

"I'm in need of a crew. I was told you could help."

I was not in need of a crew. I was in need of a way to get back to Mom and Dad and the motorboat.

The scary-looking woman tossed back her frizzy hair the way girls will when they're trying to draw attention to themselves. Except in her case, drawing attention to the scary-looking woman's frightful hair and clown lips was not what you would call a good idea. Pulling the blinds shut so as to dim the light in the room, that would have been a great makeup technique.

"Why should I help the likes of you?"

"Because I can make you rich."

"As you can see," she said, gesturing around the room, "I am already rich. Richer than any man on this island."

Sweat trickled into my eyes. "I have my eye on a prize. Not just any prize, mind you, but the devil's own."

I had picked up a few phrases while listening to some of the men seated at her bar. *Prize* was one of the words. I thought talking like a pirate might improve my chances of getting out of her office alive, so I worked it into my pitch.

"I know every cursed sailor on this island, but I don't know you, and I am loath to do business with those I do not know."

I leaned back in the wobbly chair, trying to appear more confident than I was. "Just arrived this afternoon. That's probably why you've never heard of me."

She spun and gazed out the open window onto the teal-blue water of the harbor. "You have a ship?"

"I do."

I did not.

"Out there?" She pointed out the window at the harbor.

"Yes."

She squinted. "Don't see it."

"My crew must've taken it for a short sail."

Here I was thinking of the three delinquents who stole my dory.

She redirected her gaze at me. "What be the name of the last ship you served on?"

"The *Dead Calm*."

"And before that?"

"The *Black Avenger*."

"Never heard of either. Which means they be not earners. And I'm loath to do business with them who not be earners. I need earners who can evade the Royal Navy and return with a hold so laden with gold, silver, and precious stones that the boot stripe sinks out of sight. Can you do that?"

"I can do that."

I could not do that, not really.

"What makes you different than those drunken sailors out there slurping my rum and slobbering on my women?"

"The men out there are afraid of swinging by the neck."

"And you're not?"

"If I told you that I died and came back to life and know where there's a ship with so much treasure that you'll never need another 'earner' would you believe me?"

"No."

"Then forget I mentioned it."

Sweat had started pouring down my face, stinging my eyes. I didn't dare swipe it away. I did not want her to know how scared I was.

She studied me for a moment with what I interpreted as a mixture of respect and irritation. "What sort of prize did you have in mind? Spanish galleons? French frigates? Dutch barque?"

Dutch barque is a type of ship, in case you're wondering, not some part of a tree native to the Netherlands.

"The *Nuestra Señora de Riqueza*."

She laughed. Hers was a wicked laugh. The Wicked Witch of the West laughed like this woman. Come to think of it, she *looked* like the Wicked Witch of the West.

"And how is it a young lad such as yourself intends to steal a ship from the treasure fleet and render three-quarters of its cargo to me?"

"Three-quarters?"

"How about none. Will none work for you?"

Since I didn't really intend to become business partners with the scary-looking woman I skipped the part where we negotiated shares. "I have a plan."

I did not have a plan.

"You do, do you?"

"I do."

Not really. I was only saying what I thought she wanted to hear.

"And what makes you think you could find a vessel and take it?"

"I have something the rest of those men out there do not have."

"And what pray tell could that be?"

"The dates, course, and times of the *Nuestra Señora de Riqueza's* next voyage."

"The *Nuestra Señora de Riqueza*?"

I nodded. "So do we have a deal? Fifty-fifty?" I said this mainly to make her think I knew how to negotiate with shrewd businesswomen—which I obviously did not. I'd seen my dad do the same thing, once, while haggling with a junkyard owner over a bumper for our car.

The scary-looking woman reached across the table and shook my hand. Hers was a firm handshake. A man's handshake. A handshake that hurt.

"You best know that if it be me who's putting up the crew and provisions and ship, then it be half for me. And a quarter for my crew. Expenses come out of your share. We clear?"

Her vise-like grip ground my fingers. "Deal," I said, wincing. She released my hand, thank goodness. I left her office as fast as I could. So in addition to losing the dory and having no idea what island I was on or what year it was, I had now promised to find a treasure ship for some scary-looking woman who seemed to be the island queen.

Like I mentioned before, not a great deal on my part. Some days I can be such an idiot.

CHAPTER FOUR

I Learn the Scary-looking Woman's Name

"You got tossed?"

"No. I left on my own." I was back at the gate with the strange boy from earlier. The sun had dipped below the ridge, turning the valley in front of us a purplish gray.

"Sounded like she tossed you."

"We finished our business."

"Are you really going after the *Nuestra Señora de Riqueza*?" When I looked at the boy oddly, he dropped his gaze and sheepishly tucked one dirty foot behind the other. "I was outside the window, listening."

"I only said that in order to get out of there alive. Stealing a ship would be stupid. Not to mention dangerous."

"In that case getting tossed out would have been the safer course. There is not a man on this island who would strike such a pledge with Mary Read."

THE END OF CALICO JACK

"Mary Read? *The* Mary Read. Mary Read the pirate?"

He nodded. "She's only the most feared pirate in these parts."

"What parts are we talking about?"

"Isla del Hombre Cabra. It's one of the few islands still part of the Nation of Thieves."

By *Nation of Thieves* he meant governed by pirates. This I knew from my pirate books.

The boy eyed Mom's handbag. "What's in the bag?"

I clutched it tighter to my chest. "This and that."

"May I see?"

"Maybe later," I said. "How come you're out here and not in there?"

"I, um …" the strange boy shifted nervously. "… concluded my business."

"You mean with that older woman I saw you with?"

"Yes. She is working late tonight. A fresh crew arrived this afternoon. I brought her dinner. That woman you saw me with takes care of my child."

"You're a dad?"

"Of a boy. He is only a couple months old. You cannot be too careful on Isla del Hombre Cabra. Thieves and murderers about. And kidnappers. So I leave him with people I know can protect him." The strange boy pointed at Mom's handbag. "Made from calf?"

"Yes." The two of us suffered through a few moments of awkward silence before I said, "What does Isle duh Whatever mean in English?"

"Island of the Man Goat. Scary Mary is the Man Goat. But everyone who is not a pirate calls it Isla de los Pinos because it's covered with pines. Mary will expect you to deliver on your promise. Do you have a plan for capturing the *Nuestra Señora de Riqueza*?"

"Yes."

I most definitely did not have a plan.

"You will need a captain. One the crew respects. Do you have a captain in mind?" he asked.

"I do."

I did not. On the other hand, I could not see myself leading a boarding crew of cutthroat, bloodthirsty, murderous, thieving pirates all by myself. Plus, I didn't have a ship. In case you're wondering, I had no plans to use any of Scary Mary Read's men or provisions or ship.

"I know of a captain who will help you. He has crew, a ship, and can be trusted."

"What about Mary Read? We already shook hands on a deal."

"Trust me, you do not wish to get in bed with Mary. The Devil himself would not strike a bargain with her. This captain, he will give you fair terms." Before I could protest further, the boy pulled me away from Scary Mary Read's place. "But we must hurry. You do not wish to be in the jungle at night."

Which is how I ended up following the strange boy into the jungle as the sun slipped out of sight. I had only been on Goat Man Island a short while and I'd already had a run-in with a pirate who looked and acted like Jack Sparrow and had reneged on a deal with Mary Read. So I was not having what you would call a relaxing day at the beach in the tropics.

Some days my absence seizures can take me strange places.

CHAPTER FIVE

THE CREW'S NEST

We headed down a meandering path that took us to a jungle river. The air was hot and damp and in places the terrain was more swamp than soil.

"I'm Ricky, by the way. Ricky Bradshaw."

"Andy."

"So Andy, what's Mary's story?"

"Bastard child, she was. Mary's mum lost her husband to the sea right before she gave birth to a son. Then her mum got pregnant again and had Mary. Cursed the family be, because not long after Mary came along the boy up and died. Mary's mum was afraid the grandmother would discover her son's only offspring was dead and toss her into the street, so her mum dressed and raised Mary as a boy."

"You mean the grandmother didn't notice that her grandson was a girl?"

Andy shook his head. "Happens more often than you might imagine. Girls dressed as boys. Boys dressed as girls."

I didn't know what to say to that, but I could relate. At Quiet Cove High boys claiming to be girls were now allowed to dress and shower in the girl's locker room. Same in the boy's locker room, except most of the boys didn't seem to mind girls changing in their locker room.

"Eventually the grandmother died. By then Mary's mum had squandered the old woman's estate. That's when Mary's mum hired her out as a footboy to a wealthy neighbor. First chance she found, Mary escaped to the waterfront and signed on a man-of-war as a cabin boy. There she managed to keep her secret hidden from the crew until she jumped ship."

"Is that how she ended up on Goat Man Island?"

"There were several more ports and ships and crews and a considerable amount of blood spilt but yes, she fetched up here."

Through trees ahead we saw hazy smoke from campfires in the jungle canopy. When we got closer I saw trenches in the sand from where dugouts had been pulled from the water. Far away came the faint thumping of drums.

"You sure we're safe here?" I asked.

Andy shrugged. "We'll know soon enough."

The Crew's Nest was not what you would call upscale. It would have needed thousands of dollars' worth of improvements in order to rise to the level of a decent tree house. I followed Andy up a long, meandering, swinging rope bridge that ended at what could have passed for the first level of a zip line landing. There were other landings as well, all reached by climbing ladders and ropes and, in some cases, tree branches.

A refreshing night breeze was working its way in from the harbor. Among flickering flames around campfires I saw shadowy figures of men milling about.

"Let me do the talking." Andy rapped on the door. The flap slid open. One bloodshot eye peered out at us. Andy said, "Cockswain!"

"Dance the hempen jig."
"Give no quarter."
"No prey, no pay."
"Run a rig."

The eye behind the flap shifted from Andy to me. The flap shut. The door opened. "You forgot to say 'Son of a biscuit eater,' but I'll let you pass."

Andy pushed me ahead of him, whispering, "Remember, let me do the talking."

Like I knew how to speak pirate code.

Inside I struggled to adjust to the dim candle-lighting. Loud-talking men reclined in chairs with partially clothed women sitting on their laps. Apparently there was a lack of affordable women's clothing stores on Goat Man Island.

Andy hustled me past the noisy throng and toward a back room partitioned by beaded curtains. Inside the small room round, wooden barrel casks lined one wall; a shelf at eye level was filled with dusty, amber bottles. On another wall hung a painting; opposite it an open window.

The faint light of a flickering candle revealed a man slumped forward in a chair, face turned towards us, his cheek resting on the table. Spittle glistened on his wiry beard. A brown, leather tricorn hat was pulled over his eyes. If not for the loud, gurgling snoring I might have mistaken him for dead.

"Cockswain!" Andy said.

The man stirred, lifted his head, and with the back of his hand, rubbed his mouth.

"Cockswain!" Andy said louder.

Unfocused, red-rimmed eyes toggled from Andy to me and back. "Confounded code, too many words fer my feeble mind to recall. State yer business."

"Found this lad wandering the streets," Andy said. "Escaped from the gallows in Port Charles. Wanted man. See for yourself."

Andy reached inside his pants pocket and produced a tightly wound scroll. He tossed it on the table.

In case you're wondering, right there is when I realized the strange boy was not necessarily my friend.

The man in the tricorn hat held the scroll near the flickering candle. He looked up at me, back at the scroll, at me, the scroll, me, scroll …

Andy said, "Trust me, it is him. He told me his name. I did not even have to ask."

Idiot should be my name. That's what I was thinking.

Tricorn Hat held the unrolled scroll so I could see and read. My stomach flipped and not in a good way.

While the drawing looked like something a child might sketch, there was no denying that poorly drawn sketch of a boy with tufts of hair standing straight up was me. Above the drawing were the words:

ESCAPED FROM THE GALLOWS OF PORT CHARLES
WANTED ALIVE!
dead works too
Signed: *Commodore Spotswood*

You know how, in like every adventure-spy movie, there's a scene where the good guy thinks his identity is safe and the bad guys don't know who he is but everyone watching the movie is thinking DON'T GO INTO THAT MEETING WITH THE BAD GUYS BECAUSE THEY KNOW WHO YOU ARE AND THEY ARE GOING TO KILL YOU—but the good guy does anyway? That's the way I felt.

"This you?" Tricorn Hat asked.

I said nothing. It seemed like the smart move.

"He was with a fellow who dropped it outside of Mary's," Andy said. "A local bounty hunter."

"Poor semblance, if you ask me. Not that you did." With his boot Tricorn Hat pushed his chair toward me. "Sit."

I sat.

The man extended his hand across the table. "Jack Rackham. Some call me Calico on account of the stylish shirts I wear."

His shirt was stained with slobber, sweat, and the dark, nasty swill he was drinking. I'll be honest: I wasn't all that excited about meeting the famous pirate. I'd read about Calico Jack. And what I read did not leave me encouraged about my prospects of living.

"Ricky Bradshaw."

"Happy ter make yer acquaintance, Dick."

He took a final passing glance at the sketch and tucked the scroll into the vest pocket of his coat.

"Tell me, how it be that a young lad such as yerself came ter run afoul of Commodore Spotswood?"

"I had a cellmate who promised to get me out of some trouble," I said. "But this individual claimed to be the writer William Shakespeare."

"Aye, know the sort. Liars and thieves writers be. Had a run-in with a few meself."

In the candle's light I got a better look at his face. Cheeks were sun-browned. A ragged scar ran across his chin. There was a thumb-sized patch of pale skin above his lip where whiskers refused to grow. His was the face of someone who looked for trouble and found it.

"A tale it is, then."

"I'd rather not go into how I ended up on this island right now," I replied. "Maybe later."

"Confound it all, not you. It be me who's got a tale to tell."

Confused, I glanced at Andy, who rolled his eyes. For a boy Andy had pretty green eyes.

"Ter hear the tale once will suffice. Only, this not be a yarn from them fancy books lads yer age be reading." Calico Jack drained his pewter mug and banged it on the table. "But first I'll need a fresh bottle, a fresh breeze, and a fresh kiss."

My stomach did not like the way he said *fresh kiss*. "I am … uh … not that way."

"He means me," Andy said, removing his bandana. He shook out long, brown hair and as he did I noticed for the first time that Andy's breasts were large for a boy his age and hips not simply plump, but wide.

"You're a … girl?" I stammered.

"Through and true she be," said Calico Jack.

"Happens more often than you might imagine," Andy said. "Girls dressed as boys." Andy leaned down and gave Calico Jack a sloppy kiss on the lips.

"Now then, fetch me a fresh bottle whilst I get me some good loving. When ye get back I'll tell you a tale that 'ill make yer blood run cold."

I should have run from the Crew's Nest right then.

But I didn't.

Which is how I ended up playing dirk-darts for money with Calico Jack.

CHAPTER SIX

A SEA STORY

"Out of rum," I said, placing a small amber bottle on the table. "So I got sarsaparilla. Hope that's okay."

"What sort of grog shop runs out of rum?"

"It's fine," Andy-the-girl said. "You have already had enough rum."

"I have?"

She gave him a quick peck on the lips. "Yes, love."

Calico Jack took a swig and spit it out. "This confound mash has too much bitter root."

"It'll grow on you," she said. "I did."

"So … you're a girl?"

"Anne Bonny," Andy-the-girl said to me. "Jack's first mate in more ways than one."

And with that it all sort of made sense: Mary Read, Calico Jack, and Anne Bonny. In a pirate book I'd read, all had been mentioned as having some connection to the *Nuestra Señora de Riqueza*.

THE END OF CALICO JACK

Calico Jack took another swig and belched. "Fancy a game of darts?"

I glanced around the small, cramped room. "In here?"

Calico Jack whipped out a dirk (fancy pirate word for *knife*). "Loser buys the next round."

"Where's the dart board?"

Calico Jack pointed at a portrait of a woman lounging in a meadow with goats. With a flip of his wrist he sent the dirk flying. *THUD!*

"Ye get one practice throw."

The painting was only a few feet from an open window. Though there remained a hint of light out, the air had already become noticeably cooler. A good thing, too, because Calico Jack was not what you might call a fresh flower. Which meant I turned toward the open window each time I inhaled.

"What's in that bag at yer feet?"

If Calico Jack's question was meant to distract my throwing, it worked. The dirk missed the painting—missed the wall, in fact—and stuck in a tree growing directly outside the window.

"Oh, this and that," I replied, a little embarrassed that I'd missed so badly.

Leaning out the window to retrieve the dirk, Calico Jack said, "Mind if I take a look?"

"Actually I do."

He wiggled the dirk free from the bark, turned, and before I could stop him, kicked the bag toward Anne Bonny. She snatched it up.

I lunged; she pulled back. I pulled harder and wrestled Mom's handbag from her. Right then Calico Jack grabbed me and bent back my arm.

"Give it up."

"No."

He twisted harder. "Give it."

"OW!" He had me in his grip, and I felt totally helpless as well as breathless.

"I'll snap it, swear I will."

I could feel the tendons in my shoulder stretching. There was ringing in my ears. Worst of all was Calico Jack's breath.

I let go.

"Thief," I said.

"Pirate," he replied.

Calico Jack dumped the handbag's contents on the table. There were some pretty interesting items in Mom's bag. Earrings, hair ties, bobby pins, plastic bag of breath mints, a hairbrush, pen, pencil, and some female items I won't mention.

But you know what was not in the handbag? The ship's log.

Calico Jack shifted his gaze towards Anne Bonnie. It was not the look of a happy pirate. "Where be the big surprise you said he had?"

"You saw how he guarded it," said Anne Bonny. "What sort of boy carries a handbag like that unless he is carrying something important?"

"Good point." Calico Jack pocketed Mom's earrings then tossed me the empty handbag.

At this point you may be wondering why the ship's log wasn't in Mom's handbag. I will tell you why. Andy's (now Anne Bonny's) obvious interest in Mom's handbag had not gone unnoticed by me, so while the man at the bar had filled an empty bottle with sarsaparilla, I had secretly tucked the ship's log into the front pocket of my cargo shorts.

"You have something I want," said Calico Jack.

"No I don't."

"You do. Only I don't know what it is. But figure it out, I will. Smart as paint, I be. Let's throw," said Calico Jack. He toed a scarred plank in the floor, leaned forward, and flung his knife at the woman with the goats. Its tip pierced her forehead.

"Ten points fer me."

Unfamiliar with dirk-darts, I didn't question his scoring. My throw missed the painting entirely, but at least I kept the dirk in the room.

"You were going to tell Ricky your sea story," Anne Bonny said.

"Oh, right." Calico Jack toed the line again and leaned toward the target. "Some time back we were making our way through the Windward Passage when our lookout spied a schooner. The *Kingston*, she was, with a crew of four, plus captain and passengers. For several days the *Kingston* ran the coast of Hispaniola, sailing before fair winds. Once she entered the passage, though, them fair winds changed. Narrow body of water, the passage is. Ghastly business sailing them waters."

Calico Jack threw, nailing a goat.

"Three more points fer me." He downed another gulp of sarsaparilla and burped long and loud the way a boy will sometimes when he's trying to impress those around him. (I'm not saying this is a smart move; I'm only saying boys will do this sometimes. As boys get older we grow out of this juvenile behavior and move on to farting.)

I had studied how Calico Jack threw and decided to try his approach. Holding the tip of the dirk, I bent my arm back at the elbow and flicked my wrist.

The dirk's handle hit the painting, poking a hole in it.

Calico Jack readied himself for another throw. "Was two hours before sunset when our lookout spied the *Kingston's* white sails. I gave the order to pour on canvas. I reckoned the captain of the *Kingston* must have seen us about the same time because her crew made a run fer it."

Outside our small room shouting and cursing erupted. He paused; we all looked out. A man bleeding from his nose and mouth staggered through the doorway. He crashed into Anne. Without a word Anne Bonny shoved him back out into the melee.

"Toward sunset we closed to within a league of her. When night fell her crew doused the lamps. No moon that night. No stars either. Sky and sea was as black as Davy Jones' locker."

He threw; the dirk stuck in the meadow. "Five points."

"But you hit grass!"

Calico Jack waved me over to the painting. "See that?" he asked, pointing. "Nicked her ear."

The dirk had definitely *not* nicked the woman's ear.

"No it didn't."

"The devil ye say."

"There's green grass between her and the blade. See?" I pointed at what was obviously green paint between the dirk's tip and the woman's flesh-colored arm.

"Anne, get over here." Anne Bonny joined us. "What say ye?"

"Sorry, love. You missed."

"Confound it all. Two of ye is blind as bats."

I threw again, hitting blue sky.

"Nothing fer sky," said Calico Jack. "But yer aim be getting better."

On his next throw Calico Jack picked up two points for drilling a flower.

On my third try I speared a goat.

"Three points?" I asked.

"Not fer that goat," said Calico Jack. "I already hit that one."

"You're making up the rules."

"I'm afraid Jack is correct," Anne Bonny said. "A wounded goat gets you nothing."

On Calico Jack's next attempt, he threw underhanded and—miracle of miracles—harpooned the exact same goat I'd hit.

"One point."

"But you just said no points for a wounded goat!"

"Wounded, no. But a dead goat is worth a point. Three blows to a goat and the goat goes off the board."

"This is a stupid game."

"Yer only saying that 'cause yer losing." Calico Jack straightened the painting and continued with his story. "At first light I gave the order to crowd on sail."

"He means his attack on the *Kingston*," Anne Bonny explained.

I rolled my eyes in a way that suggested I knew that already.

"Soon as we was in range we sent a shot across the *Kingston's* bow. Surprised was I to see the captain hove to. I reckoned he seen we meant business and ran up the white flag. We came alongside and let down two gigs. Armed with muskets, pistols, cutlasses, and knives we rowed over to take command. Was less than five lengths away, we was, when the fool captain ordered his crew to fire on us. Musket balls tore into our gigs. Sank one. Nearly scuttled the one I was in. Lost good men, I did."

The bloody and beaten man from before staggered into our room.

Looking nervously about, I said, "Perhaps we should finish this game later when people aren't fighting."

"That squall will blow itself out soon enough," said Calico Jack. "Jest men letting off steam, is all."

With a grunt of annoyance, Anne grabbed the man by his shoulders, spun him around, and sent him reeling back into the fray; his jaw connected with a fist and he crumpled to the floor.

With his next throw, Calico Jack nailed a goat's horn. "Fifteen points."

"For a goat horn?"

"Horns be hard to hit. Count fer more. Once the crew aboard the *Kingston* seen our gig taking on water they began cheering and yelping. Hearing them crow like that got my blood to boiling. Came on fast, we did, killing two right away.

Rest of 'em got chased down in quick order. While I was taking stock of the situation one of the passengers aimed a pistol at my head and pulled the trigger. Gun flashed in the pan. He went fer his dirk, but I laid open his forehead with my cutlass. I grabbed the poor lubber and hauled him ter the rail. Asked my crew if I should throw the whimpering lubber overboard, but my crew thought that the man was too well dressed to dance with the devil, so we tied him to the foremast with ropes so tight his hands turned the color of plums."

"Why are you telling me all this?"

"I be trying ter give ye the lay of things, Dick, so ye can strike your colors."

"Strike my colors?"

"Decide whose mast ye will stand before."

"I have to stand before a mast?"

"Loyalties, mate! Loyalties! A crew with a rebellious spirit 'ill mutiny in a skinny minute." He chugged more and belched in my face. "My crew took a dirk and stabbed it through the man's fine broadcloth coat. Sliced downwards from neck to navel, the way a butcher marks a section he's about to hack out. A shower of banknotes fell from the man's coat onto the deck. Every man grabbed all he could, shoving them notes inter pockets and caps. Found the captain's mate, a mangy mutt infested with fleas, in a food locker. Cut out the dog's tongue, I did, and flung him over the side. Swum for a minute or more, yapping as best it could. Then, the water slashed white, and a big shark took him down." Seeing the stunned look on my face, Calico Jack grinned. "Sharks have ter eat, same as men."

From outside our room a shot rang out, followed by a scream. More shots, more screaming, followed by yelling and furniture breaking.

"Had some fun with the captain and crew. Hauled one up the foremast and used him for target practice. Nailed the boatswain's feet ter the deck and his arms ter the tiller.

THE END OF CALICO JACK

Blindfolded another and made him kneel in front of the small swivel cannon. Poor feller's head exploded like a melon."

Trying to block out the grisly mental picture Calico Jack painted, I aimed carefully at the painting and nailed the woman in the belly.

"Worth five points," Anne Bonny said.

I could not imagine why stabbing the goat woman in the belly would get me points but it felt good to finally be on the board.

Calico Jack threw but missed the painting entirely. He blamed it on the cross breeze blowing in through the window, but I suspected it was the rum. "I made a bed of oakum and tied the captain over it. Then we stuffed more oakum into his mouth and soaked it all with turpentine. I did the honors and laid the torch to it. The captain burned briskly, he did, his howls drowned by our laughter."

"You burned him alive?"

"The man wasn't forthcoming with the truth. There's a price to pay for dishonesty, Dick. Remember that." When he said this he eyed Mom's empty handbag. I think he was sending me a message. "Sailed the *Kingston* back here."

As unbelievable as it sounds the bloodied, beaten, and now toothless man from before tumbled into our room again.

"We had a right lovely time," Anne Bonny said. "Right up until the point where some bounty hunters from Port Royal trapped you in a cove and stole the *Kingston* from under us."

"Hate a bounty hunter," said Calico Jack.

The beaten and bloodied man held his gut as blood spurted from between his fingers. A crimson stain spread across his white shirt. With a blank look, he dropped to his knees, and face-planted. Anne Bonny nudged him with her boot. The man did not react.

"Dead?" said Calico Jack.

Anne Bonny nodded. "And there is fresh crew about, love. We need to—"

Before she could finish Jack Sparrow burst through the doorway swinging a cutlass like a madman. "I'll gut you LIKE A grouper!"

Calico Jack went for his dirk on his hip … and realized it was in the painting.

The crazy bounty hunter helicoptered his cutlass in the air like a ninja warrior.

Anne Bonny backed away, leaving me by the table all by myself.

A split second later Jack Sparrow's cutlass *whooshed* past my backside. That was all the motivation I needed. I dove out the window and hit bark with my face. (I think I mentioned that the Crew's Nest was like a huge tree house, which meant the tree literally grew right next to the window.) With me hugging its trunk, my feet searched for branches, a rope, anything to keep me from falling.

Nothing.

Jack Sparrow leaned out and swung the cutlass, intending to decapitate me.

I let go and fell.

CHAPTER SEVEN

Rapids Development

What happened next only lasted a few seconds, but it seemed a lot longer.

First I hit the ground.

Only before I hit the ground I bounced off tree limbs, ropes supporting the swing bridge, and hammocks stretched between branches and landed on top of a passed-out drunk, so it helped break my fall. A bunch of other drinking men rushed over and pulled me off their friend. While I was still lying there, Anne Bonny rushed down from the Crew's Nest and into the clot of men leaning over the passed-out drunk. I think she meant to help me, but by this point I had managed to crawl my way through legs and over bodies and reach a scrub bush. I watched while Anne slapped and clawed and pushed men away who were pawing at her.

More drinking men—apparently thinking there was a scrum-fight breaking out— charged the drunken clot of men.

THE END OF CALICO JACK

At that exact moment Calico Jack ran toward the scrum pile, his frock flapping behind him and his wild, oily hair flying back. He held a dirk in his teeth, cutlass in one hand, and pistol in the other.

From high above, Jack Sparrow launched himself out the window. I suppose he intended to replicate my Superman-like dive.

Unfortunately for Jack Sparrow, the scrum of drinking men, Calico Jack, and the seriously flattened drunk had moved out of the way. Jack Sparrow hit with a *thud*!

I don't mind saying, I was a little bit happy about that.

I realize all this sounds pretty unbelievable—individuals falling from two stories up and no one getting hurt (except Jack Sparrow, which was okay with me). But it happens. Not often, but sometimes. Like in 2014 there was a window washer who fell eleven stories and landed on the roof of a car. He broke his arm and had some injuries to his side, but he lived. I'm not saying you should try this. I repeat: I AM NOT SUGGESTING YOU JUMP FROM YOUR TREE HOUSE. I'm only saying it's possible to fall two stories and land on people, and survive. That's all I'm saying.

Without waiting for Anne Bonny and Calico Jack, I sprinted toward one of the dugouts I'd seen beached next to the river. My plan was to take the dugout and escape. I had made a deal with Scary Mary Read to steal a treasure ship. And now Jack Sparrow, Calico Jack, and Anne Bonny intended to turn me in to Commodore Spotswood for the reward on my head. So running away from famous and dangerous pirates seemed like a great plan. But before I could paddle away, Anne Bonny joined me in the dugout, then Calico Jack.

So that was a problem.

"Think the guy who is trying to kill me is dead?" I asked.

If you think I was making idle conversation or concerned about Jack Sparrow's health you are mistaken. Here I was thinking about saving my own neck.

Calico Jack gave a final look back at the twisted, crumpled, flattened figure that was Jack Sparrow. "Doubtful. But I'm pretty certain he broke sumpin'. Leg or arm or neck."

"That won't stop him," said Anne Bonny. "I know men like him. Married one. I would still be with that scoundrel if not for Jack."

Jack Sparrow or not, I got out of the dugout. I wasn't about to remain with a pair of famous pirates—even if Calico Jack had taught me how to play dirk-darts.

"Where do you think you're going?" said Calico Jack.

"Home. Hotel. Some place without pirates."

"The devil ye say. Yer coming with us. Ye have something I want."

"No I don't."

"What does he have that you want?" Anne Bonny said this while still carrying Mom's handbag, which, if you will recall, did not have the ship's log in it. "Aside from the reward, he is not worth all that much."

"You told me he be going after some sort of treasure." I'm sure my eyes bugged out at this accusation. "Check his pockets," said Calico Jack. "Maybe he has a treasure map." He rushed me, threw me to the ground, and felt around until he found the bulge in my cargo shorts' front pocket. "What's this?" he asked, holding up the ship's log.

"Nothing." This I said with my face pressed into the dirt. Which meant nothing came out sounding like *nuffun*.

His weight lifted from me. I rolled onto my back and watched him flip pages.

"Appears to be a ship's log of some kind."

"It's not."

THE END OF CALICO JACK

"Says right here *SHIP'S LOG*, see?" I didn't bother to look; I knew what it said.

"That is probably from the vessel he mentioned to Mary. I bet that is the treasure ship's log, love. *Nuestra* something another."

"*Nuestra Señora de Riqueza*."

"Yes, that one."

"Sign on with me and let's be finding that ship together. I'll help ye stay clear of that bounty hunter back there."

"Told you I would find you a captain and ship and crew," Anne Bonny added.

"I've changed my mind. I'm not interested in becoming a pirate and finding that treasure ship."

"Dick, Dick … I not be asking."

thwaat!

An arrow sank into the side of the dugout.

"Best grab a paddle unless you wish ter be tonight's main course."

"Main course?"

"Cannibals," said Calico Jack, pointing up. "In them trees."

Darkened figures, holding bows and arrows, sat on branches. I started paddling.

"Paddle faster!" Anne Bonny said to me.

I was already paddling pretty fast, but with arrows whizzing by my head I found a whole different gear.

"Shoot, love! Shoot."

Calico Jack loaded his pistol, aimed, and … nothing. Cursing, he complained about a jammed jiggermebob.

Thud! Thump! Thwatt! Arrows and darts stuck fast. Our dugout began to look like a pincushion.

Ahead of us came roaring—roaring like you might expect to hear if you are, say, on a white water rafting trip and heading toward falls. Which is exactly what we were doing.

crack!

40

A spear lodged itself into the floor of the dugout, opening a seam about a half-inch wide. Half an inch may not sound like much, but in an old wooden dugout that is already loaded with people, it was a huge deal.

Water poured in.

More arrows stuck.

Another spear went *THUNK!*

The dugout turned, tipped, and flipped.

So there I was flailing around in the midst of rushing rapids with natives chucking spears at me and shooting arrows and you want to know what I was thinking? I was thinking: OH NO! THE SHIP'S LOG WITH THE *Nuestra Señora De Riqueza* COURSE IS GETTING SOAKED!

Right then my face hit a humongous rock in the river.

I blacked out.

CHAPTER EIGHT

Trapped

"Bad news," I heard Calico Jack saying. "We lost the ship's log."

I came to on wet sand. Twilight had turned into night. Animal sounds filled the jungle. The roaring of the river seemed louder in the dark. Far away savages were beating their drums. This I heard while still on my back and my head pounding from a killer headache. In a game of rocks, rapids, and skulls, rocks win every time.

Anne Bonny stood over me, gently slapping my cheek. "We don't need the ship's log," she said. "We have the boy. He can lead us to the treasure ship."

"I can?"

"Can ye will. On yer feet, Dick. Need ter get ter me ship and fast."

I stood; we all three approached the river, and waded in. This time I covered my face as I floated downstream.

THE END OF CALICO JACK

An hour or so later I came drifting into the harbor in the dark all alone. Calico Jack and Anne Bonny had left me in their wake. But I only needed to dog paddle and listen. From across the harbor came cursing and stammering, which I took to be Calico Jack complaining about something or other. Following the string of profane utterances I found his vessel and pulled myself up the anchor rope.

"We're trapped," said Calico Jack, not offering his hand to help me aboard.

I flopped over the rail and landed on my back, relieved to be out of the water.

"Trapped how?" Anne Bonny said.

Calico Jack pointed behind us. "See that huge Spanish warship gliding into the bay?"

We all looked at the huge Spanish warship gliding into the bay. Even in darkness I could tell there were huge cannons poking out of its side. What Calico Jack neglected to mention—or maybe hadn't noticed—was that the warship was towing a sloop.

"We be out of reach of her guns for now, sitting behind this island like we be. And the water's too shallow for her to enter. But I wager that captain has recognized old Jack's brigantine as a pirate ship and he'll be wanting to maneuverer his vessel so as to block our escape."

"So what's the plan?" Anne Bonny asked.

Calico Jack turned to me. "What be the plan, Dick?"

In the few seconds we had been talking, the Spanish warship did exactly as Calico Jack said it would and maneuvered to obstruct the channel.

"Looks like they have decided to settle down and wait until morning," I said. "They have time and we obviously aren't going anywhere."

"That's not a plan," Anne Bonny said, as if I needed reminding.

"Weren't you the quartermaster on Charles Vane's ship when he slipped through the blockade put around New Providence?" I asked.

Now Anne Bonny was the one with a bug-eyed look of surprise. "How did you know that?"

"I read a lot." In one of my pirate books there was a whole chapter on Anne Bonny and Mary Read. The chapter on Calico Jack was shorter.

"Quartermaster I was. What of it?"

"You know things. Pirate things. How to steal things."

"I be knowing things too," said Calico Jack.

"Not saying you don't, but she didn't cheat at dirk darts and didn't beat me up while stealing from me. Her I trust more. Not a whole lot more, but a little." I dropped to one knee. "Here's what I think we should do." Drawing imaginary lines on the deck, I told them my plan.

"It will never work," said Calico Jack.

"It might," Anne Bonny said.

"It better. Else there be the devil ter pay," added Calico Jack. "And I be the devil."

Under the cover of darkness, while Calico Jack's brigantine rode quietly at anchor, the three of us swam toward the Spanish warship. I floated beneath the stern of the great ship, watching to make certain lookouts didn't see the pair, while Anne Bonny and Calico Jack scrambled aboard the British sloop. I endured a few anxious minutes of waiting, before I saw Calico Jack on the sloop waving me aboard.

"Any trouble?" I asked.

Calico Jack nodded in the direction of bodies—four of them, throats slit—fallen like cordwood on the deck. "None now."

His comment made me regret ever coming with Anne Bonny to the Crew's Nest.

"Dick, ye not be troubled by any of this, are ye?"

I swallowed hard. "No sir."

"Good. 'Cause pirating be bloody and messy."

On Calico Jack's orders Anne Bonny cut the sloop's anchor cable. With no lanterns lit and the sloop riding on a gentle breeze, we rode a falling tide out past the other end of the island. In darkness the big warship grew smaller until it was gone. My plan had worked: we'd stolen the British sloop from a Spanish warship.

Which officially made me a person wanted by Commodore Spotswood, Jack Sparrow, a tribe of indigenous natives upset over the theft of their canoe, and the Spanish Armada.

Which meant I was not feeling all that great about the prospects of ever seeing my parents again.

CHAPTER NINE

A Nation of Thieves

"We're about to enter treacherous waters." That's what Anne Bonny said to me when she came on watch at sunrise.

Not: "Thanks for keeping us on course all night while Jack and I slept."

Not: "Steering by compass and stars without a chart is not easy for someone doing it the first time."

Not: "Good job, Dick."

Instead she said: "You are going to want to head a little more to port unless you want to run this ship aground."

"What makes these treacherous waters?"

Her wild tangle of curls flew off her shoulders, the ends brittle and stiff from salt and wind. Bug bites marred her skin.

"See how the colors change from deep blue to light? That means shallow water. Keep an eye out for reefs and coral heads. A smear of brown water means reefs … or a coral head."

You know what was weird? Calling the stolen British sloop a *ship*. I have seen bigger floats in Christmas parades.

"Oh, and grassy bottoms may look like brown water but it may not be all that shallow."

I said, "How will I know the difference?"

"I doubt you will."

From below came banging and stomping interrupted every few seconds with a rattling hacking cough.

"That would be our captain stirring," Anne Bonny said. "Sounds like he survived another bout with the bottle."

"It's none of my business, but he seems to drink a lot."

"Pirate." She stated this as if no other explanation were needed. "Pirates are drunks with a sailing problem. He has tried to stop. Has, in fact. Numerous times. But he always ends up pulling the plug from the jug."

On a northerly course we chased small white clouds across a brilliant blue sky, sailing on a broad reach with a following sea. The stolen British sloop sliced through the swells, moving away from Goat Man Island and the danger that was sure to follow. I had no doubt Scary Mary would send men to find me. Anne Bonny had made that clear.

"Mary will want payment for her time and effort," she explained. "If she does what I heard you tell her, she will have put together a crew for you by now. And probably located a vessel. Mary does not take kindly to those who double-cross her."

We had a substantial head start, but I wondered if it would be enough.

With one hand on the ship's wheel I anticipated the pitch and dip of the sloop. To the east the sun blazed bright over the horizon.

"Where exactly am I sailing to?"

"Spanish Wells."

"Why not New Providence?"

"Long story."

I took in the scenery. Except for a few specks of land on the horizon, the scenery was water. "Seems to me we have time for a long story."

For several minutes we sailed along in silence before she said, "After Charles Vane was voted out as captain of the *Ranger,* Jack took command. Not long after, they attacked the merchant ship he spoke of last night, the *Kingston*. They sailed to Isla del Hombre Cabra to hide out and spend their fortunes. But as he said, a bounty hunter tracked them down. While Jack and his men were ashore, that rascal took possession of the *Kingston* and the *Ranger*, leaving Jack and his men stranded."

"That's a pretty shade of blue over there." I pointed towards light-teal-colored water. "Should I head that way?"

"Only if you want to run aground. Water that color means there is white sand close below."

"Oh."

"Vane might have been too careful a captain for the crew's liking, but he never lost the *Ranger*, not like Jack. The crew disbanded. Most headed north toward New Providence to take advantage of the pirate pardons the governor was offering. Jack waited until things settled down and then stole a good-sized sailing dory. He and three others set out for Nassau. Took them nearly three months. That's when I met Jack."

The hull hit hard, shuttered, bumped, and bounced. Before I could react, Anne Bonny grabbed the helm and pushed it hard over. The sloop tipped onto its side, sails full, and continued on.

"Run aground in these waters," she said, "and there will be the devil to pay."

"Got it," I said, unnecessarily. "Avoid brown water, green water, teal water, and stay in the dark-blue water … if I can find any."

"Sometimes it helps to squint. Makes it easier to distinguish between colors."

I tried. Squinting did not help.

"When I met Jack I was married to James Bonny, a loathsome individual. Jack offered to buy my freedom, but my husband would have none of it. So we made the decision to hire ourselves out as privateers. Jack assembled some of his old crew, explaining that privateering was like pirating, only legal. But of course once a pirate always a pirate. His crew demanded that we all go back to pirating or be voted out as captain. The ringleader of the group was Mary Read. I cannot say that Jack was reluctant to return to his former ways. He chafes against authority. We captured a few vessels near Bermuda, several off the Carolina coast, but none worth noting. By that point I was expecting with Jack's child, so we made our way back to Isla del Hombre Cabra."

"Aren't you worried about leaving your child?"

"The boy is better off without me. When he is older the woman in whose care I left him will see to it that he is sent to Bristol for his education. I pay her well, with the promise of more as long as the boy does not ever discover that his mother is a pirate-whore."

"But you seem to like pirating."

"I like the thrill of the hunt and the prize that follows. Jack likes his rum. No doubt both of us will die as pirates."

For a few moments we sailed in silence. I savored the feel of the rough wood beneath my feet, the smell of salt air, and the way the waves lifted us each time we crested a swell. All those nights I'd stared out the window of my bedroom at the *Virginia Pride*, I'd never really believed I'd come to command a ship of my own. Certainly not a pirate's ship.

"Isn't Spanish Wells near Nassau?" I said this thinking I might impress Anne Bonny with my geographical pirate land knowledge.

"Yes, but me crew is in Spanish Wells," said Calico Jack, stomping his boots on the deck as if to announce his presence.

"With luck, we will come in under the cover of darkness," Anne Bonny said.

I was about to mention that so far we had not had very good luck when Anne Bonny said, "Ah, love. We have company."

Calico Jack and I looked to where she pointed.

"Ten degrees off port," she said.

He raised the spyglass to his eye. "Spanish warship. I dare say it be the one what had this sloop. See fer yerself."

With the spyglass she studied the vessel for a few seconds, then said, "How did they find us? And so soon?"

"Little matter does that make," said Calico Jack. He glanced around the horizon as though weighing his options.

Anne Bonny handed me the spyglass. Through the curving rainbow rings of color I saw a white rectangle sail low on the horizon against a vast sea of blue.

"Should we set a course for George Town?" Anne Bonny said.

"Ne'er make it. Got the wind of us, she does."

With the glass to my eye, I saw three corners of the topsails. No question that she was a three-masted ship: and a large one. She had two gun decks with the blunt snouts of cannons sticking out.

And we had one pistol.

"It is clear we'll not outrun her on this tack," Anne Bonny said.

"Or any tack," said Calico Jack.

He stroked his wiry beard, then looked up at our sails. Shifting his gaze toward the brown water to the west, he said to me, "Fall off to port and make speed. We'll take our chances in the shallows. There not be a warship in these parts that can navigate these shifting shoals and reefs."

Anne Bonny asked, "Can we?"

THE END OF CALICO JACK

"Love, it be Jack yer talking to."

Of course at that very moment we ran aground.

Which is how we ended up stuck on a shoal with a Spanish warship bearing down on us.

CHAPTER TEN

Hard Aground

The little sloop turned into the wind, bouncing hard on the shoal. Calico Jack loosed its lines, causing the sails to luff noisily.

"Confound it all, I hate a grounding. Whose fault is this?"

"Mine," Anne Bonny said.

"No it's not. It's me," I said. "I was on the helm."

"Well, one of you two better get us off and fast."

Even as he said this, the warship fired an opening volley. The shot splashed harmlessly in the water behind us, but the message was clear. We were dead in the water and soon to be blown out of the water.

Which was pretty much what Calico Jack said.

"Ship that size will have two hundred crew or more, all armed. Most likely she'll simply keep her distance and fire broadsides until we're blown out of the water."

"Surrender?" I asked. It seemed like a rational option.

"Never! Better to die before the mast than with a rope around your neck."

Another volley splashed right next to the sloop. A second followed quickly, then a third.

Anne Bonny jumped into action and began throwing things overboard: steamer trunk, stool, pots, plates, a crate of bananas.

"What the devil are you doing?" said Calico Jack.

"Lightening our load," Anne Bonny replied. "You two could help."

Calico Jack remained where he stood. "Ye be wasting yer time."

"Says you," Anne Bonny shot back.

I began tossing stuff over the side. Almost immediately the hard shuddering that ran the length of the hull lessened. Next Anne Bonny and I tossed the small table we used to eat on. It landed upside down and floated away in our wake like a four-posted raft. Several more items sailed over the side and then … miracle of miracles, the sloop shifted, slipped off the shoal and righted itself.

"You're welcome," Anne Bonny said tersely.

Without waiting for orders, I sheeted in the lines while Calico Jack spun the ship's wheel. Instantly the little sloop heeled over and accelerated.

"Dick, take the helm. I'll guide you."

"Are you mad?" Anne Bonny said. "You cannot possibly expect to sail through those coral heads and over that reef."

"Trust me, I know what I'm doing." Hurrying to the bow, Calico Jack leaned over and guided me with hand signals. "Dick, follow my lead."

BOOM!

A splash of exploding spray soaked him. Ahead, streaks of white foam broke across coral heads, turning the greenish water brown. Calico Jack pointed first one way, then the other. I followed his signals. Below us the crunching sound of the hull raking across coral grew louder, the vibration beneath my feet, harder.

"Jack, if you're not careful you will break her spine."

BOOM! BOOM!

Spray and bits of coral splattered onto the deck. A sudden and violent vibration jerked the helm from my hand.

"Now you've done it," Anne Bonny said. "The rudder is stuck fast."

I released the ship's wheel and let it turn freely. On the rush of an approaching swell the small sloop skipped and, grinding its way forward, moved on.

"Jack, we're in less than four fathoms."

"We'll make it."

"Three!"

"Trust me."

BOOM! BOOM! BOOM!

"TWO FATHOMS!" Anne Bonny called.

"It's more than two, love."

"Not by my eye it isn't."

The sloop struck hard: a single sharp impact that turned into grinding that ran along the length of the ship, until the vibration beneath my feet lessened, then stopped. Calico Jack regained his balance and turning back to us said, "Yer welcome."

Off we sailed into the sparkling sea, the coral heads growing smaller below our keel as the reef's shelf fell away.

The booming continued, only now that we were out of range of the warship's massive guns, the eruptions were behind us and less frequent.

"What now?" Anne Bonny said.

"We make for Don't Rock Bay."

"That warship is not going to give up and turn around," Anne Bonny said.

THE END OF CALICO JACK

"Well aware of that I am. And I also know it cannot come the way we did. Dick, here, will come up with a plan, ain't that right?"

"I'll try."

"Ye'll do better than try. Else there be the devil ter pay. And the devil be me."

CHAPTER ELEVEN

Don't Rock Bay

"**B**efore we hear Dick's great plan fer putting leagues between us and them Spaniards, let's drink to my great navigational skills."

"Too late. The rum is gone."

"The rum is gone?"

"Yes, the rum is gone."

"Why is the rum gone?"

"For one, because it is a vile drink that turns even the most respectable men into complete scoundrels. Two, that reef back there nearly broke the spine of this vessel and would, no doubt, had I not lightened the load. And three, it makes your breath stink."

"The rum is …?"

"Gone. As is our food, water, bunks, and those shells you kept under the floorboards."

"YOU THREW OUT MY SEASHELLS?"

Anne Bonny gestured toward the warship growing smaller in the distance. "You're welcome."

"BUT WHY? WHY WOULD YOU THROW OUT MY SHELLS?"

Anne Bonny glanced my way and rolled her eyes. "Maybe you can explain it to him."

I shrugged but said nothing. It seemed like the smart move.

By the time I sailed us into Don't Rock Bay the sun was falling. Calico Jack had assured us the Spanish warship would not attempt to enter the small bay, and he was right. The vessel remained well offshore.

"Drop anchor!" Calico Jack shouted.

The crew (Anne Bonny and me) did as ordered.

"I'll take the first watch," Anne Bonny said. "Love, you take second."

"How come Dick can't take the second watch?"

"The boy sailed us through the night and all day. Love, let him sleep a few hours."

I went below and stretched out on the floor where my bunk would have been if Anne Bonny had not thrown it over. There was only one small problem and the problem was this: when I woke up Calico Jack would expect me to have a plan for how to escape the Spanish warship.

And I didn't have what you would call a detailed plan.

I had the beginning of a plan. That was all I had. No middle or end.

Which meant I'd owe that devil Calico Jack.

I woke with a start. "Get up," Anne Bonny whispered to me. I opened my eyes. The interior of the sloop was dark.

"Go out the forward hatch," she continued in a hushed voice. "Climb over and swim ashore. Don't come back. Not ever."

Carrying my shirt, I crept forward and crawled up through a forward hatch. When I peered back I saw Jack talking to someone, but it wasn't Anne Bonny. I couldn't make out exactly who it was, but the silhouette of the person looked oddly familiar. It did not leave me with what you might call a good feeling. Slithering on my belly toward the side of the little sloop, I peered down at the water, raised up on my elbows to slip over, and …

The cold, sharp blade of a knife pressed against my Adam's apple.

"Move, even a little, and I'll gut you like a grouper, you stupid guppy. Savvy?"

Hearing Jack Sparrow's voice so close, so warm, and his breath not what you would call minty fresh, made me twitch.

Which is how I came to have my throat cut by a cutthroat pirate.

CHAPTER TWELVE

HELD FOR RANSOM

Not all the way cut.
 But enough to cause a small amount of blood to trickle down my chest. This was Jack Sparrow's way of making sure I followed his instructions. And his instructions were for me to march myself to the back of the sloop.

The five of us gathered at the back of the small British sloop: Calico Jack, Anne Bonny, Jack Sparrow, Scary Mary, and me.

"You owe me," Scary Mary said to me. "He owes me," she said to Calico Jack and Anne Bonny. "The boy vowed to bring me the *Nuestra Señora de Whatever*. Said he was an earner, he did. Instead he tucked tail and ran like the coward he is."

In the short time it had taken me to walk from the front of the boat to the back with Jack Sparrow's knife pressed to my throat, I had come up with the threads of a new plan.

"If it be the lad ye want, take him," said Calico Jack. "He's of no value to me."

He was lying, but he sounded convincing.

I stood at the helm wearing nothing but damp cargo shorts, my sodden shirt still balled up in my hand. Though the night air was warm and humid, I still shivered.

"Jack, Jack, did you not notice?" Scary Mary said. "That be the same Spanish warship you stole this sloop from. It not be just the lad they want."

"You wouldn't turn against yer old captain?" said Calico Jack in a tone that sounded more hopeful than confident.

"Would. Have."

Scary Mary pivoted so she could direct her gaze at the ship parked on the horizon. In the black of night with only the stars' glow for light, the massive ship appeared to radiate with an orangish glow. "The captain and crew be anxious to square matters. Seems the captain took a fancy to this sloop. Had plans, he did, of sailing it around Jamaica with his missus."

"Come on, let me gut the boy like a grouper," Jack Sparrow pleaded.

"Not now," Scary Mary replied. "First there be the business of a treasure ship to find."

Calico Jack rubbed his wiry beard as though considering his options. "How 'bout if Anne and me agree to split our shares of any prize we find with you. What say ye ter that?"

"I say that be bold talk for a tired old man on a lee shore. How about if I take the lad and this sloop? In return you and Anne get that dory we come in. I'll give you a day's head start. Perhaps it'll be enough to keep the two of you from swinging from the gallows. Doubtful, but maybe."

"The lad could be lying about the treasure ship," said Calico Jack.

"He's right. I could be lying." It seemed like the right thing to say.

I should point out that the blade of Jack Sparrow's knife remained pressed against my throat, so saying even those few words were painful.

"If he be lying he be dying," said Scary Mary.

"Let me put the thumbscrew to him," Jack Sparrow said. "I love using the thumbscrew."

"I already know you lost the ship's log."

"How could you know that?"

"Trees talk," Scary Mary said, smiling.

"Natives," I offered.

"So what be your plan for finding the *Nuestra Señora De Whatever*?"

"It's not exactly a plan so much as an idea of a plan."

Scary Mary got right in my face—got so close our noses and lips almost touched. Which only made her even scarier.

"Dick, here, mesmerized the route," said Calico Jack. "Didn't ye?"

"He means memorized," I said.

"And told me some of it," said Calico Jack.

I had not, but I understood why Calico Jack said this. He was looking for a way to keep from getting cut out of the deal.

"This plan of yours," Scary Mary said, her face still inches from mine. "Does it include you living? Because right now your prospects of living seem scant."

I gulped. Which caused Jack Sparrow's knife to slice a little deeper into my skin.

"You better tell her your plan," Anne Bonny said.

"It might not work," I said.

Scary Mary rested her palm on the blunt edge of Jack Sparrow's knife and pushed ever so slightly, moving her hand back and forth a little. "For your sake it better work."

So I told them my plan for finding the *Nuestra Señora de Riqueza*. Which wasn't so much a plan as recounting of the history of Calico Jack, Anne Bonny, and Mary Read's last days as West Indies pirates. Readers are leaders and at that moment I became the leader of our small band.

CHAPTER THIRTEEN

MY GREAT PLAN

"It will never work," Scary Mary said.

Anne Bonny replied, "It might."

"It better," said Calico Jack. "Else there be the devil ter pay."

"And you're the devil, I know," I said.

"Let me gut him like a grouper … please."

"Would you please shut up?" Scary Mary.

Calico Jack, Anne Bonny, and Scary Mary all turned their gaze back toward the Spanish warship glowing orange on the horizon with its lit lanterns.

"What are the odds this will work?" asked Jack Sparrow.

"Long," said Calico Jack.

"Dangerously long," Scary Mary echoed. "But that matters little to you." This she said to Jack Sparrow. "You stay with the sloop."

"The devil you say. I'll do no such thing."

Scary Mary boxed Jack Sparrow's ear, then flicked his forehead with her finger. "No backtalk. I hate backtalk."

"But you can't leave me?" Jack Sparrow said, rubbing his ear. "Them Spaniards will kill me when they find out the four of you escaped."

"A small price to pay fer our freedom," said Calico Jack. "'Sides, if the captain really has his heart on sailing to Montego Bay with his mistress, like Mary says, he'll be pleased as rum punch ter get back this sloop. And with a galley slave ter boot."

"But it's so unfair," Jack Sparrow complained. "There's no food, no water. I'll starve to death."

"Stop your bellyaching. Them Spaniards will rescue you by morning," Scary Mary said.

"Dick, bring the sailing dory around to this side. I'll hold her close while the three of ye pile in."

"It's not fair. I found the boy," grumbled Jack Sparrow. "I'm due a bounty."

Minutes later, under the cover of darkness, Calico Jack, Anne Bonny, Scary Mary, and I sailed away in their small dory, leaving Jack Sparrow still complaining that he was being left out of our great plan.

"Your plan better work," Calico Jack whispered to me.

"Trust me, it will."

I knew it would not.

CHAPTER FOURTEEN

Preacher's Cave

After a rough night passage from Don't Rock Bay I had finally settled on a plan to escape. My plan was this: run away as soon as we made landfall. But with three of history's most notorious pirates holding me hostage, that didn't seem like a really great plan. So I came up with a second plan to escape: lead them to the *Nuestra Señora de Riqueza*. *Then* run away.

My thinking here was that by capturing a ship laden with silver from Peru and Mexico, gold and emeralds from Colombia, and pearls from Venezuela, my three captors would be distracted long enough for me to disappear without them noticing.

A couple of things had me worried. How exactly were we going to capture the *Nuestra Señora de Riqueza*? We didn't have what you would call a big pirate ship with cannons. And our crew so far was four: me, Calico Jack, Anne Bonny, and Scary Mary Read. Not exactly great odds for capturing a Spanish galleon.

While I was thinking on how to improve on my plan to run away, I got some bad news, as if I needed any more.

Calico Jack called out, "Sail ho!" (Pirate term for *LOOK! THERE IS A BIG SHIP!*)

We all looked. The tops of two masts appeared on the horizon behind us.

"Make fer that island," said Calico Jack. "And be quick about it."

By island he meant an enormous blackish-gray rock the size of the Dallas Cowboys Death Star Dome. From my perspective the Dallas Cowboys Death Star Dome rock looked like a meteor that had splashed down in the middle of a wide body of shallow, blue water.

"You think sailing to that island be wise?" Scary Mary said. "The water appears shallow."

"Only them that knows it can navigate these waters. That be why I picked the Preacher's Cave fer me crew's hide out."

I did as Calico Jack ordered and tacked toward the wall of jagged cliffs that I was certain we'd crash into. I said as much. "If I keep on this course we'll crash into the big rock island."

"Difficult ter see, lad. Won't spy the cut until you're practically on it."

Less than fifty yards from hitting the Dallas Cowboys Death Star Dome rock, I spied a blind pass between two rocks. The cut couldn't have been more than thirty yards wide.

Calico Jack dropped the sails. The current was wicked strong, but with the four of us pulling oars we made it through. Moments later we were through the long, narrow cut and ghosting along on calm water smooth as Astroturf. It was like we were in an atoll, except the Bahamas don't have atolls. Volcanoes form from atolls. And volcanoes formed the islands of the West Indies. The Bahamas do not have volcanoes, so they do not have atolls.

That's probably more information than you wanted to know.

The island-that-was-not-an-atoll was beautiful beyond description. In the landlocked harbor there was a perfect circle of white beach with water so clear you could not tell where dry sand stopped and water started. A high, rock-ribbed dune sheltered us from the trade winds blowing out of the east. Beyond came the distant roaring of surf. To the west were high cliffs so tall no ship sailing across the water could have seen the mast of our small dory anchored in the cove. Coconut palms ringed the beach, and beneath them grew lilies and sea grape bushes. Best of all were the numerous large caves that looked out from the bluffs, any one of which could have housed a crew of pirates.

"Good ter be home," said Calico Jack. "How my soul has missed this place."

Anne Bonny leaned her head on his shoulder, tucking her arm in his. "Being back does make me want to settle down and think about starting a family."

"But love, we already have a family."

"I know. Perhaps I should reconsider sending Little Jack to Bristol."

"The two of you need to get a room." In the morning's light, with her black frizzy hair standing straight up from a night of wind-blown sailing and still dressed in her black velvet vest, black blouse, and black trousers, Scary Mary looked even scarier than before.

"Don't worry," Anne Bonny said to Scary Mary. "You'll find love someday."

"I certainly hope not."

Following Calico Jack's orders, I beached the dory.

"Best go see what the boys have been up to since we've been gone."

THE END OF CALICO JACK

With everyone grabbing a side we dragged the dory clear of the water and above the high-tide line.

"I don't see another vessel," Scary Mary said, stating the obvious.

Anne Bonny said to Calico Jack, "Where is the schooner you entrusted to the crew?"

"Probably beached someplace fer repairs. There be plenty of shallow beaches for keelhauling, with good trees for rigging block and tackle to snake a ship over on her side."

Scary Mary grabbed Calico Jack by the collar of his frock. "Do not tell me we sailed all this way and you do not have a ship?"

"I'm sure the boys have her tucked in a hidey hole someplace. Let's head up to the Preacher's Cave. I be anxious ter hear the details of Dick's plan fer capturing that treasure ship."

At the words "details of Dick's plan" my stomach jumped—and not in an *I'm excited* sort of way. The exact details of how we were to capture the *Nuestra Señora de Riqueza* were still fuzzy. My plan was basically this: fit out a ship for treasure hunting, and surprise the *Nuestra Señora de Riqueza* at some specified day and hour and longitude and latitude to be determined. That was as much as I'd told them. But if any part of my not-so-detailed plan failed, the three bloodthirsty pirates had promised to slit my throat.

Except for that, it was a beautiful day in the Bahamas.

I wish I could accurately convey the striking impression I felt when I entered the Preacher's Cave that looked out over the cove. Like the slit of an enormous, almost closed eye, the mouth of the cave swept in a low arch more than fifty feet wide. It had to be at least ten feet high in the center, with crawling rooms leading away from the large chamber. Once inside, the ceiling rose to a height greater than I could reach.

There was evidence of campfires beneath the two chimneys that reached upward to reveal the morning's azure sky, but we didn't see any men lurking about. A flock of bats, disturbed by our careless approach, fluttered out of one.

"Where be your crew?" Scary Mary said.

"Yes, love, where is everyone?"

"Beats the devil out of me. Confound it all, they be here when I left."

Scary Mary said, "How long ago was that exactly?"

"Not sure. A while."

There was a dry rattling as several crabs, bodies large as grapefruit, scampered away sideways. In dim sunlight, we felt our way to the back of the cave. I half expected to find a human skeleton, its molding fragments mingled with the scattered bits of crab shell and rat bones.

"I know it's none of my business, the three of you being pirates and all," I said, "but is it possible that your crew got captured? Or signed on with another ship?"

"They would die rather than hang," said Calico Jack. "Loyal to the death they be."

"And yet the place appears to be deserted," Scary Mary said, once more stating the obvious.

"The boys probably be out having a little fun, is all. Probably off raiding a turtle trader or —"

"SURPRISE!"

And surprised we were to turn and see men charging at us.

CHAPTER FIFTEEN

A Not-So-Happy Pirate Birthday Party

From dark shadows shabbily dressed men rushed forward and surrounded Calico Jack.

"Happy Birthday, boss," said a tall, muscular pirate who looked liked Charlton Heston from the 1990 version of *Treasure Island*.

"It's not my birthday," said Calico Jack.

"No? When is your birthday, boss?"

"Not sure. One of them months that has an R in it, I think."

"*Birthday* has an R in it. Come on, boys, a song for our fearless leader."

"Happy Birthday to you
You live in a zoo
You look like a monkey
And you smell like one too."

"How sweet. Your crew is throwing you a pirate birthday party," Anne Bonny said.

The men gathered around and clapped Calico Jack on the back like he was a long-lost friend.

"Ladies? Dick? Allow me ter introduce you to my crew."

Calico Jack pulled a scruffy-looking fellow forward. "This here be … what be yer name, again?"

"One-Tooth Tommy Earl."

One-Tooth Tommy Earl had the boyish appearance of a younger Justin Bieber. He kissed the hand of Anne Bonny, then Scary Mary's. I kept my hands in my pockets.

"Right." To another he said, "and you are . . .

"Gunner John 'Old Dad the Cooper.'"

More hand kissing. More of me keeping my hands in my pockets.

One by one Calico Jack's crew stepped forward to introduce themselves.

"Black Eye Patch Baker."

"Grinning George Fetherston." Grinning George did not have any teeth, which left him with something like a permanent smile.

"Fearless Fenis Fenwick."

"Richard Corner Pocket."

"Little John Davis."

"Little John Eaton."

"Little John Cole."

"Not So Little John Howell."

"Patty Cake Carty."

"Noah Hardwood."

"Thomas Bourn Brown." If you guessed that Thomas Bourn Brown was of African descent you guessed right.

"Thomas B. Quick."

"Big Ben Palmer"

"Edward 'Bilge Swill' Warner."

"Sir Walter Rouse."

"Big John Hanson."

"Big John Howard."

And so the introductions went until finally Scary Mary said, "Where be Jack's ship?"

"Ship?" Charlton Heston made a face like he had just bitten into a rancid prune.

"Yes, ship," she said. "That thing you sailed here on?"

"Oh, that." Charlton Heston dropped his gaze and tucked one dirty foot behind the other. "We, ah … sort of … lost it."

"You lost my bloody ship? Where? When? How?"

Charlton Heston scrunched his face as if in deep thought. "Can you ask the question slower, boss?"

"Where … did …. you … lose … my … ship?"

Charlton Heston pointed out the cave.

"Yes, yes, but where out there? How far away?"

"Oh, not far," Charlton Heston said excitedly. "Less than a mile."

"When exactly?"

Charlton Heston's face scrunched up, again. "Let me think …" He cut his gaze towards the clot of men standing with him, as if hoping one of them might help him with the answer.

"Was day before yesterday, wasn't it?" said Old Dad the Cooper.

"That's right!"

"How did you lose it? Wreck on a reef? Run up on a sandbar?"

Charlton Heston shook his head. "We was boarded, boss."

"By pirates?"

"Can't say. Captain what took it made us swear an oath and promise we wouldn't say anything to you 'bout it."

"But you jest did," said Calico Jack.

"Hey … not fair, boss. You tricked me."

"What be the name of the scoundrel who took my ship?"

"Don't remember, exactly," Charlton Heston said. "Tim Beers."

"No, that weren't it," Thomas Bourn Brown said.

"Captain Greenwood?" All the pirates shook their heads. "Forest Stump?" Charlton Heston said hopefully.

"He means 'Woodes Rogers?'" Scary Mary said.

Charlton Heston frowned. "If you knew, how come you asked?"

"Let me see if I have this right," Scary Mary said to Calico Jack. "Are you telling me that Woodes Rogers, the first Royal Governor of the Bahamas and the man sent by the Crown to rid the West Indies of pirates has captured your flagship?"

"I am not saying anything of the sort." Calico Jack pointed at Charlton Heston. "He said it."

"But he is part of your crew, right?"

"I guess."

"And he does seem to be their leader."

"The boys voted to put me in charge," Charlton Heston said. "I am humbled and honored."

"Can we go back to something you said a moment ago?" I said to Charlton Heston. "You mentioned something about an oath. What sort of oath?"

"To stop pirating. They said if we swore an oath, our crimes would be plunged to the depths."

"He means expunged," I said.

"That one. We did. They did. And here we be."

"How, exactly, did they let you go?" I asked. "Did they give you gigs to use?"

Charlton Heston shook his head. "Floats."

"What sort of floats?"

"Wooden casks. But they was empty. We didn't exactly get any of the rum we was promised. Bobbing around like we was, we liked to never made it back here."

"Don't tell me you headed straight for our hideout?"

"Okay."

"Okay, what?"

"I won't tell you."

Calico Jack covered his face with his hands and, shaking his head, mumbled a few more bad words.

"Ah, love? You're going to want to see this." Anne Bonny had wandered back to the mouth of the cave and now stood looking out at the cove where we had left the dory.

"Not now, love. I be contemplating how many lashes ter give this imbecile."

"But it's important."

"Forty be too few. Four hundred 'ill most likely kill him."

"But we have company."

"Company? What sort?"

"Of the British soldier sort."

We all rushed to the mouth of the cave. First one gig, then another and another and another entered the small cove. Eight British soldiers sat in each gig, six with rifles resting on shoulders. Two others worked the oars.

Calico Jack clapped his huge hands on my shoulders and squeezed so hard my stomach did a double somersault. "I reckon now be the right time for you to tell us yer plan for escaping them British sailors what's coming fer us, Dick." Leaning his face close to mine, he whispered, "And it better be a good one."

"My plan?"

"Yer the brains in this outfit." He squeezed my shoulders so hard my arms started going numb. "And I be the muscle."

So I told them my great plan for saving Calico Jack's crew from the British sailors.

Which was really not all that great of a plan.

Or original.

THE END OF CALICO JACK

But one time on TV I had seen the plan work, so it was worth a shot. And if it didn't work there would be the devil to pay.

CHAPTER SIXTEEN

My Great Plan for Capturing a British Warship

"It will never work," Scary Mary said.

Anne Bonny replied, "It might."

"It better," said Calico Jack. "Else there be the devil ter pay. In fact, I be thinking it time ter give the devil his due."

"What do you mean?" I said.

"Toenails."

"Toenails?"

"Mine need a trim. Seeing as how yer the low man on the mast, I designate ye as my pedigreeist."

"He means pedicurist," Anne Bonny said.

As if I couldn't guess that one myself.

"But not right now. Later," said Calico Jack. "Once we be out of this fix."

THE END OF CALICO JACK

Charlton Heston said, "What do you want us to do, boss?"

"When them soldiers get here and ask, you tell them you found that dory washed up on some rocks. Don't say a word about the four of us being in here, got it?"

"Aye, aye."

Calico Jack got into the face of Charlton Heston, which thankfully meant he was no longer breathing his sour breath into mine.

"Do this right and there might be an extra share of the prize in it fer you. Do it wrong and heads 'ill roll. And I mean yers." He turned to the clot of men. "To stations, boys, and be quick about it."

Within minutes two campfires blazed bright, smoke wafting up each chimney. The aroma of food cooking, indescribably delicious, filled Preacher's Cave. Fish and conch, lime and leek sizzled on skillets.

"Careful, men," warned Calico Jack in a hushed voice.

The heads of British soldiers appeared over the cave's ledge. Very slowly they climbed up and in, surrounding the six pirates huddled around the two campfires. The pirates, three in each group, did not seem alarmed by the soldiers. Rather they continued to cook and eat and laugh and tell raunchy pirate stories, burp, and fart.

"Is that all of them?" Calico Jack whispered to Anne Bonny.

"I count thirty-two."

"In that case . . . NOW, BOYS!"

The remainder of Calico Jack's crew burst forth from their hiding places.

Bats scattered. Soldiers whirled, reached for weapons, and . . .

You know that scene in *The Wizard of Oz* where three guards jump the Tin Man, Lion, and Scarecrow? There is a fight out of sight where straw flies with some yelling? And when it's over the Tin Man, Lion, and Scarecrow end up wearing the guards' uniforms? You know that scene?

It was like that only different.

There was a blur of arms swinging and fists hitting faces and cutlasses whirling about. Within moments the thirty-two British soldiers were naked except for their skivvies. Calico Jack's crew bound the soldiers' hands and feet, doused the campfires, and, leaving the soldiers inside Preacher's Cave, sealed it shut with palm branches and small rocks to make it appear abandoned.

Dressed as British soldiers we rowed out of the small cove and toward the great warship anchored in deep water.

I leaned toward Anne Bonny and said, "I have a bad feeling about what's about to happen next. Perhaps we should turn back."

"It'll be fine," Calico Jack replied. "My men are well schooled in deck fighting. Them soldiers, they'll come at us with rapiers. A rapier be lighter and can easily slip between a man's ribs or shoulder blades, but the proper weapon for this fight is the cutlass. When it connects it'll do damage and worse. Why, by thunder, a slicing swing that hits where it ought, just below the chin, be almost certain to decapitate the poor fellow. Trust me, Dick, we'll escape this scrape jest fine."

I wasn't so sure. I had not participated in the action back in the cave, but Calico Jack had made it clear he expected me to do my part once we boarded the warship.

As Calico Jack predicted, we reached the warship during the start of the afternoon watch. A few of the crew hailed us, waved, then went about their business. Dressed in British sailor uniforms we appeared to be no threat, though if the sailors had looked more closely they would have seen an unwashed, unshaven crew.

Calico Jack's men clambered aboard, swinging cutlasses, and mowing down sailor after sailor. I'm not going to describe the gruesome manner in which the British sailors died, only to say, it sickened me. Movies and TV make light of death by showing it too often. In real life watching someone die violently causes a normal person to vomit.

Which, of course, I did. But out of sight so the crew wouldn't see me.

Within minutes the heavy cutlasses began to take their toll. Cornered and outnumbered, the few sailors on deck dropped their weapons. Calico Jack ordered one of the British sailors to go below and find the captain. As Jack had said would likely be the case, he was off watch eating his midday meal. When the captain appeared on deck, Calico Jack brought the full force of his cutlass flat-side against the man's skull, driving him to the deck. Two of Calico Jack's crew helped him into a sitting position.

"May I?" Scary Mary said. "Him I recognize. We have a history."

"Have at him," said Calico Jack.

"Order those men of yours who are cowering belowdecks to drop their weapons and come up one by one."

"I will do no such thing."

With a shrug, Scary Mary cocked the hammer of her pistol as if to blow his brains out.

"Wait! I have an idea." I'll be honest: I was terrified. The plan for taking the British warship was mine and if we got caught it would probably be me who Woodes Rogers would hang first.

"Wouldn't it be quicker and easier if we smoked them out?"

"Good thinking," Anne Bonny said.

Torches were lit and dropped into open hatches, which were then sealed shut. Moments later fists began pounding on the hatch covers. The pirates stood around laughing and pointing as the crackling of fire and men's screams grew louder.

I had no desire to see anyone shot or stabbed or burned to death because of my plan, so I said, "Probably should let them out before we burn up the ship."

"Good thinking." Calico Jack ordered one of the hatch covers lifted. Sailors poured up from below.

He was about to order them shot when I said, "Better have your men hurry to put out the fire. Otherwise she'll burn to the waterline."

"But what about them?" said Calico Jack, pointing at the sailors diving overboard.

"You have the ship. That's all that matters."

He shrugged. Then he shot the captain.

The whole affair was over in short order.

"See?" Anne Bonny said. "I told you Dick had a good plan."

"Smart as paint he is," said Calico Jack.

"All we have is a British man-of-war," Scary Mary said. "And that only because your crew lost your ship. What about the prize that's due me?"

"Let's meet in the captain's quarters, so Dick can plot a course for the … whatdidya say the name of that ship is?"

"*Nuestra Señora de Riqueza.*"

"That one. But 'fore we do that, there be the small matter of my toenails. Dick, let's you and me head to my quarters fer that pedigree. "

CHAPTER SEVENTEEN

WE PLOT A COURSE FOR A TREASURE SHIP

"We are within striking distance of the *Nuestra Señora de Riqueza*. I am certain of it."

I was certain of no such thing.

The four of us had gathered for a conference in the captain's quarters. An unrolled chart lay before us showing the blunted shoreline of North America and the West Indies and different longitudes for a good many crudely drawn islands, reefs, and headlands. Some of which I recognized.

I thumped my finger on the square due east of Jamaica and west of Hispaniola. "Right here, I'm positive."

"Tell me true, she'll be there?" Calico Jack, admiring his pedicure, rested one large, dirty foot on the edge of a chair.

I stood upwind of Calico Jack's dirty, smelly feet. My handiwork had improved the appearance of his toenails but did nothing to address his foot-odor problem. "In three days the *Nuestra Señora de Riqueza* will be on a northerly course along this longitude."

THE END OF CALICO JACK

To be honest I had remembered some of what I'd memorized after tearing out the pages in the ship's log. Not all, but enough. So once I saw the map, some of the plotted numbers came back to me. Problem was the time. I didn't know what day it was, what year it was.

And I wasn't about to ask.

"No time to lose," said Calico Jack. "We make sail at dusk."

"Why not now while we have the sun at our backs?" Scary Mary said. "That'll make it easier to read the water."

"Don't want to raise suspicions. A ship at anchor in the Devil's Backbone be not likely to be of a concern to them on shore."

"As long as you don't run aground," Anne Bonny said not-so-lovingly.

"Now love, you know me better than that." Calico Jack rolled up the chart and tucked it in a hole cut out of a beam in the cabin's ceiling. "And the course we steer be not east, but west. Sailing into the sun is dangerous business in these waters."

"West?" Scary Mary said.

"Our fortunes lie in Nassau. Now then, time for old Jack to get some shut-eye. Dick, I'm putting you in charge of getting this vessel shipshape. Boil vinegar and scrub the deck. Can't have them bloodstains fer all ter see when we pull into port."

"But I was hoping to catch a nap. I haven't slept at all since … well …" Here I was thinking of how I had just drifted off to sleep the previous night when Anne Bonny had awoken me. "… a long time."

"You can sleep when I say so. No rest for the bleary."

"You mean weary," Anne Bonnie said.

"Same thing."

Which is how I ended up on my hands and knees scrubbing blood and brains off the British man-of-war's deck all by my lonesome.

Some days being a pirate is no fun at all.

CHAPTER EIGHTEEN

NASSAU

As we tacked our way into Nassau harbor, I savored the warm, moist air rattling the man-of-war's sails. Behind us, to the east, clouds tinged with pink banked against a deepening purple sky. Just ahead lay a beach of white sand and pink coral. Small breaking waves marked the outer fringes of the large island. Palms grew inland as far as the eye could see. We had arrived in Nassau, the pirate capital of the world.

Or it had been until Governor Woodes Rogers arrived.

I knew some of what lay ahead: we needed more crew and a different vessel, one built for shallow waters, so we could escape into coves as necessary. Calico Jack and his men would see to the crew and selection of a ship. It was left to me to find a surgeon.

Once the anchor splashed, Calico Jack said to Charlton Heston, "Guard the ship. See trouble, shoot it. Keep shooting 'til the trouble retreats, dies, or you're dead. At the first sign of trouble, sound the alarm."

"What be the alarm, boss?" Charlton Heston asked, sounding woefully ill-prepared for the task. "You didn't tell me the signal."

"Three bells will start me running. I doubt I'll get back in time ter save you, but at least those of us on shore will know there be trouble aboard."

I looked across the wide band of water crowded with ships and the cluster of sails strung between palms. A rowdy group of men was milling about on the beach not more than a hundred yards away. Campfires had begun to blaze. Some sang drinking songs and not very well.

With my palm resting on the butt of the flintlock pistol I had been issued, I said to Calico Jack, "Should I stay here too?"

This was my feeble attempt to get out of my assignment.

"No, Dick. Ye head over ter that speck of land and find us a surgeon who knows how to wield a saw, pull teeth, sew flesh, and pluck eyes as necessary. If ye can find one with his own barbiturates, the better."

"I'll do my best."

"I know ye will, Dick." He clamped his hand on my shoulder and squeezed hard. "Anything less than yer best be not an option."

The flintlock pistol's long barrel rested heavy against my thigh, secured only by a hemp rope holding up my cargo pants. (I'd lost my belt. When and where, I couldn't recall.)

Standing on the deck of a British warship with a flintlock pistol tucked into my waist and wearing only faded, tan cargo shorts secured by a rope, a red bandana around my head, and a Ron Jon surf shirt with holes in the arm pits, I certainly looked the part of a pirate.

Charlton Heston and I helped the others lower three gigs over the side, then watched as Calico Jack and his crew paddled away.

"I know a surgeon," Charlton Heston said.

"You do?"

"Crewed with him, I did. Take me with you. I'll take you to him."

"You heard the captain. You're supposed to stay here."

"Nobody will know."

"I'll know. Besides, the captain trusts me to do this by myself."

"What if I take the gig and leave you here?" Charlton Heston said.

I should mention here that Charlton Heston had pulled out his dirk and, while he wasn't actually threatening me, I could read his body language. And his body language said, "I'll gut you like a grouper."

"Okay," I said.

"Okay, what?"

"Take the gig. Go find your surgeon. I'll stay here and guard the ship."

Charlton Heston studied me for several seconds, his face bunching into a frown. "It's a trick, isn't it?"

"No trick."

It really was not. I wanted out of the task of finding a surgeon. Charlton Heston taking my place seemed like a win-win for both of us.

"I see what you're doing. You want me to take the gig and go."

"Well … yeah, sure. That's what you want too, right? I mean, it was your idea."

"How do I know it was my idea? Maybe it was your idea," Charlton Heston said. "Maybe you put that idea in my head."

I didn't have a response to that so I said nothing.

"I see what you're doing," Charlton Heston said. "You want me to go ashore and as soon as I do you'll sound the alarm, Jack will come back, find me gone, and heads will roll, starting with mine."

THE END OF CALICO JACK

"I won't ring the bell, I promise."

"Like I'm going to believe the word of a lubber. Take the gig! Go! I hope you get rolled in an alley by hooligans."

"Really, it's fine," I said. "I don't mind staying behind."

"Get!"

So I did. I lowered the gig (without Charlton Heston's help), waved goodbye, and paddled away.

By the time I reached shore and tucked the gig in some marshy reeds, the sun was below the western sky. Livestock pens and small garden plots lined a footpath leading inland toward ramshackle buildings. Looking east, then north, I turned west, and off I went to find a surgeon.

CHAPTER NINETEEN

HOBBLING DOBBIN

I picked my way among a crowd of people pushing wooden carts until I found a tavern. It was a bright enough little place illuminated with torches. The board over the door was newly lathered with red paint. Thick black letters let me know I'd found The Dung Heap.

The windows were open to catch what breeze there was. Red curtains fluttered. The floor was sand. Open doors, both wooden and large, funneled the breeze in from the front and out the back. The customers were mostly seafaring men, and talked so loudly that I hesitated to ask the crowd at the door.

"I am … ah … looking for a surgeon. Do you know where I might find one?"

A man in the door looked me up and down. Without changing his unpleasant expression, he waved me in.

At the bar I said to a man seated on a wooden cask, "I'm looking for a surgeon to crew for a spell. Know where I might find one?"

"Who be asking?"

I offered him my hand. "Ricky Bradshaw."

He tipped his tricorn hat. "Paddy One Boot."

"One Boot?"

"Had an unfortunate encounter with a ball of lead."

He hiked up one pant leg. I expected him to reveal a wooden stump, but he had both limbs, only his left foot was black and swollen like an overripe grapefruit. Cloth strips stained with some kind of nasty-looking pus oozed through the fabric.

"Gangrene?"

"Aye. Green it was. Don' recall the first name of the chap what shot me. Doc says me foot needs ter come off, but I'm disinclined ter part with any flesh, even if it be black and rank."

"So you know of a doctor?"

"Aye. Hobbling Dobbin. But ye won' find him in here, no sir. And ye won' find him on any ship of the likes ye aim ter sail either."

"How do you know what sort of ship I sail?"

"It be in yer eyes, mate. Ye have the look of a lad going after a prize and in need of a man of medicine who can bandage and sew and saw. If I be wrong, tell me plain and yer first drink be on me."

First off, I wasn't about to have a drink in such a place. And second, he had read me like a book. "You might try dropping some silver coins in a tub of seawater and swirl it around. Sometimes silver can help draw out an infection. At least that's what I've read."

"If I had silver I'd buy me enough rum ter make this cursed pain go away."

"I can get you silver."

"Can you, now?" I nodded. "How much silver?"

"Much as you want. Provided you can lead me to this Hobbling Dobbin fellow," I said.

Obviously, I wasn't going to give him as much as he wanted. It wasn't mine to give. Plus, giving Paddy One Boot any silver would require us to capture the *Nuestra Señora de Riqueza*. And while I had told Calico Jack, Anne Bonny, and Scary Mary that it would happen, I was not sure *how* to make it happen.

"Give me yer hand," Paddy One Boot said.

"Why?"

Paddy One Boot snatched my right arm by the wrist and pulled my hand towards him. Before I could stop him, he whipped out his dirk and sliced a long, deep gash across my palm.

I almost screamed like a little girl. Then I remembered I was in a tavern filled with swarthy, muscular men who would possibly kill me for reacting like a wimp, so I bit my lip and shut up.

He did the same to his own palm and with me still staring at my bloody palm slapped his on top of mine, pressing our two hands together.

"Deal sealed in blood, it is now. Yer word be good as gold. And if ye don't deliver, the devil himself will come fer my share."

"But you still haven't told me how to find Hobbling Dobbin."

He stood, hitched his pants up, and limped towards the door leading out into the night. "Ye jest did, mate."

CHAPTER TWENTY

Is The Good Doctor In?

"You're the doctor?"

"Aye, that and more."

"But why do you call yourself Paddy One Boot?"

"Fer effect. And respect. It wears on me better than Hobbling Dobbin, which be my Christian name. Born John Patrick Dobbin, me was, but I ne'er liked that name, so as a boy I had folks call me Paddy. Then this business with me foot came up."

"But you are a doctor?"

"Aye. Trained under the best, I did. Have me own kit and tools and barbiturates."

"So why not tend to your own foot?" I asked.

"Doctors be the worst kind of patients. Ever' time I prepare meself for the treatment I pass out. That might partially be due of the rum and barbiturates, though."

"I could do it."

"Do what?"

"Apply the treatment. With your help, I mean. It would be like I was your assistant."

"But wouldn't it hurt jest the same?"

"You tell me. If I give you some of the powders in your bag, will you feel anything?"

"Not fer a while, I won't."

"Then I say we try to save that foot. Where's your office?"

"Lad, it's Hobbling Dobbin yer speaking to. I makes house calls, I does. And ship's calls. But an office?" He gestured around the tavern. "This be the closest thing ter an office I ever had."

"In that case let's head to my gig. It's tucked in a safe place. We'll have plenty of privacy there."

I didn't say this to Hobbling Dobbin, but here I was thinking that if he screamed, a lot fewer people would hear if we were down at the marsh area.

Minutes later I had Hobbling Dobbin lie on his back in the bottom of the gig. He hugged his crutch to his chest the way a child might clutch a teddy bear.

"How much do I give you?" I asked.

"Start with a little. It be powerful. And expensive. But if I get ter moaning during the procedure don' hold back."

I will not go into all the gory details of how I had to keep putting dabs of pitch under my nose to kill the stink, or how I peeled back layers of dead, black skin, or how in some places actual bone poked through. I'll skip all that. Let's just say that after almost an hour of plucking and swabbing with seawater and applying ointments, Hobbling Dobbin's foot was markedly improved. I cut strips of cloth from a shirt and wrapped the foot.

Then I waited for him to wake up.

And waited.

And …

From across the harbor came the clanging sound of bells ringing. They chimed loud and fast. Which meant Charlton

Heston was sounding the alarm. Which meant he was in trouble. With Hobbling Dobbin moaning and groaning and reaching for his foot, I paddled as fast as I could toward the man-of-war.

There came a gunshot, followed by a second and third. *POW, POW.*

Then came a splash.

Which meant the British sailors had retaken the man-of-war … and Charlton Heston was dead.

CHAPTER TWENTY ONE

WE STEAL THE *WILLIAM*

"You brought me a crip fer a surgeon?"

I knelt beside Hobbling Dobbin, holding the gig close to a piling. Calico Jack's crew had gathered on a dock at the edge of the harbor.

"Says he trained under the best."

"Is he dead?" said Scary Mary. "He looks dead."

"I gave our surgeon a little something to help him sleep while I worked on his foot."

"Did you cut it off?" said Calico Jack. "Looks like ye cut it off."

"No, but I might yet." To be honest, I didn't like thinking or talking about fixing Hobbling Dobbin's foot, so I changed the subject by asking, "Did we lose the British warship?"

"Yes. That part of your plan worked."

"And the next part better work as well," Scary Mary said.

At this point I should mention that none of the crew seemed too concerned that Charlton Heston's body, having floated over with the current, floated facedown next to the gig. They certainly made no attempt to retrieve it.

"Them British soldiers will be raising all kinds of hell trying ter make sense of what happened aboard. Eventually they'll check the log, see where she last lay anchor. They'll back track ter see if there be any survivors. That be when we make our move."

"What is our move?" Anne Bonny said.

Calico Jack turned to me. "Tell 'em the plan, Dick."

"It's best if I share it only with you," I said. "In case, you know, others get ideas of challenging you for captain."

"Smart as paint, yer are. Seen that right off."

So I leaned close and whispered the plan to Calico Jack.

"Well?" said Scary Mary.

"Dick says we're going to steal that ship." He gestured down the dock at an impressively large vessel.

"The *William*?" Anne Bonny said. "Love, have you lost your mind?"

"She be agile, fast, and carries one hundred guns, making her a force to be reckoned with."

"And what makes you think we can walk up and take that ship without anyone saying a word?" Scary Mary said.

"Tell 'em, Dick. Tell 'em what ye told me."

"The plague."

"What about it?" Scary Mary did not give off would you would call a confident vibe.

Here I nudged Hobbling Dobbin to make sure he was still warm. Satisfied I hadn't killed our new ship's surgeon, I gathered his vile bile of dead flesh.

"What died?" said Calico Jack.

"Him," Anne Bonny said, pointing to Charlton Heston.

"No, something else be rank."

"I'm gonna puke," Little Elton John Eaton said. And he did.

"That dead skin is our ticket to that ship," I replied.

Calico Jack said, "Well, keep it downwind, would ye?"

With the men clamping their hands over nose and mouths, I doled out assignments to the crew.

"It will never work," Scary Mary said.

Anne Bonny replied, "It might."

"It better," said Calico Jack. "Else there be the devil ter pay. In fact, I be thinking it time ter give the devil his due. Me hair needs a wash. Think I got mites. Scalp itches something awful. Seeing as how yer the low man on the mast, I be thinking ye can be my mortician."

"He means beautician," Anne Bonny said.

"Yeah, that one I got." And with that we went to work spreading the plague.

CHAPTER TWENTY TWO

THE BLACK PLAGUE

First one, then another of Calico Jack's crew climbed up the lines holding the *William* to the wharf. Slowly they made their way into position. Calico Jack, Anne Bonny, Scary Mary, and I watched from my gig, well away from the ambient light of the ship's lanterns. The rest of the crew had used their gigs to encircle the ship and sneak aboard.

Hobbling Dobbin groaned, moaned, and reached for his foot. Anne Bonny shoved some powders into his mouth, then whispered, "Night, night."

Minutes passed before a shrill whistle split the silence, followed quickly by a deckhand yelling, "THE PLAGUE! BLACK DEATH!" With dead flesh flaking off Calico Jack's men, the *William*'s crew leapt over the side and swam to shore. A few hesitated on the beach, pointing at the *William*. But when one of them saw the sodden strip of flesh I had placed on the neck of Charlton Heston, all broke and ran toward the

THE END OF CALICO JACK

shops and pubs, warning of the deadly outbreak that was sure to spread and kill every inhabitant in Nassau.

Within minutes Calico Jack and his crew, with me leading the way, boarded the *William*. Soon the anchor was up and dripping sea grass off bow chocks. Sails began to draw, catching the night breeze, and sending the *William* east in our hunt for the *Nuestra Señora de Riqueza*,

"Dick! Remember to bring a nit-pick. And the lye soap."

While the campfires on Nassau's beach grew dim behind us, I went to work washing Calico Jack's hair. Some days it doesn't pay to be a pirate.

CHAPTER TWENTY THREE

Calm Before the Storm

There is a moment before unforeseen tragedy strikes when everything seems right in the world. From the first day we had moved into that apartment across from the marina, I had spent hours watching as the crew of the *Virginia Pride* went about their business on deck. I had savored the smell of gunpowder when her cannons boomed on the Fourth of July and listened with reverence to the heavy thumping of cannon wheels rolling over wooden planks. The night our apartment building burned down, I swayed back and forth ever so slightly to the imaginary pitch and roll of the *Virginia Pride* as she sliced through waves.

And now, though it was still dark out, I stood on the deck of a real ship, enjoying her lift and fall as she sliced through the waves. Looking east, I searched the horizon for the thin, red line that marked the onset of a new day—my first as a full-fledged pirate. I won't go into the business of how I picked out the mites, shampooed Calico Jack's greasy hair with lye soap, and oiled his dry scalp to prevent dandruff. I'll skip all that because right then the man in the crow's nest sang out, "Sail ho!" (Fancy pirate phrase for, *Hey, would you guys napping on deck wake up and pay attention!)* "Twenty degrees to port!"

In the distance against the dark, gray sea, I could barely make out the vessel's darkened shape. For several seconds I stared. Then, as the almost imperceptible light of day began to bleed across the water, I spied a mizzenmast carrying a large sail, cupped and full, pulling her away from us.

From atop the mast the lookout called, "She's spotted us. Pouring on canvas, she is!"

Springing to the helm, Richard Corner Pocket called, "How do you make her?"

Men, startled by the sudden cry, sprang to the ship's rails.

The lookout answered, "On the starboard quarter, hull down, sir."

At this moment Calico Jack appeared on deck, and climbing into the rigging, surveyed the sail through the glass. Sweeping his scope around the horizon, his gaze settled on a particular point on the horizon. "Let fly the topsails!"

"Let fly the topsails!" roared Thomas B. Quick.

"Aye, aye, sir–r–r!" answered the men. The men sprang into the rigging and went aloft like cats. Instantly all was a bustle on board the *William*. The topsails were unfurled, while on deck men set about the heavy work of sheeting the halyards.

Swinging himself down on the deck by the main backstay, Calico Jack came to where I stood. "Pay close attention, Dick. I'll be 'specting ye to take charge of this crew if need be."

"Oh … kay," I said, unsure what to say to that bad news.

In a few seconds the *William* shuddered as the sails filled and snapped. Then, rolling gracefully onto her rails, she cut through the waves as Calico Jack directed her course toward the prize.

In no time we had closed the gap by half.

"From the clumsy appearance of her masts and sails I judge her to be a trader," Thomas B. Quick said.

"Aye, and heavy in the hold," replied our captain.

When we were within a mile we hoisted Calico Jack's flag, the one he had brought from Goat Man Island for just this occasion. Up went the flag, the crew giving a rousing cheer.

Receiving no acknowledgment from the captain of the trader, Calico Jack said, "Fire a shot across her bow!"

In a moment the *William* was a blur of activity with men removing large sections of the deck amidships. In the hole now before me, cannons were rolled into position, barrels thrust out through small openings. One was quickly loaded. A crewmember worked a swivel and elevated the barrel.

"On my order!" Calico Jack called.

The men on the gun sighted down the cannon's barrel.

"Fire!"

The cannon boomed.

Its heavy ball struck the water a few yards ahead of the trader, splashing it as the vessel sailed into the spray. Knowing almost nothing about firing a cannon or how to aim one, I found myself stunned that the gunner could so easily eyeball the target and come that close without actually hitting the ship.

"You watch," said Calico Jack. "She'll back her topsails, now, and hove-to."

I watched and waited, as did the other men. Sure enough, within moments the vessel's crew furled her sails, allowing the *William* to draw closer until we were only about a hundred yards off.

"Lower the boat!" said Calico Jack. "Dick and me will go over and have a word with the captain."

"Me?"

Calico Jack shot me a look. It was the sort of look that suggested the devil would be expecting another payment soon.

THE END OF CALICO JACK

I'll skip the boring part about how we paddled over, except to say that I was surprised at the sight before my eyes on the captured vessel's deck.

Instead of a crew of sailors, as expected, there were nine dark-skinned men, standing on the quarterdeck, looking at us with stunned expressions. They were totally unarmed, not to mention mostly naked. One wore a pair of trousers cropped at the knees. Another wore something like a towel over his privates. He also wore a brown pelt Davy Crocket hat. The most ridiculous was the chief, a tall, bearded man with a deeply seamed face, and thick crop of tightly coiled white hair. He wore a smug expression, as if he had been expecting us. He also wore a white cotton shirt, a swallowtail coat, and a straw hat. If not for the color of his skin, he could have passed for Mark Twain.

"Who's the commander of this ship?" said Calico Jack.

"I is," Mark Twain replied, removing his straw hat and making a low bow.

"Where are you sailing from and where are you bound?"

Mark Twain pointed back over his shoulder. "Dat way." Slowly he turned and pointed ahead. "An' dis way."

Calico Jack gave me a look that let me know he didn't think the chief was all that smart. "What sort of cargo are you carrying?"

"Cocoa-nuts, conch, turtles."

"That's it? That's all the cargo you carry?"

The chief shrugged. "Does our best, we do."

Calico Jack grunted. "Yer best be sorely lacking." Holding his flintlock pistol toward me, Calico Jack said, "Kill them."

"Wait! What?"

"This trader be worth more than some turtles and conch. We can raid twice as many vessels with two ships. Do it."

"That's murder."

Calico Jack placed his strong, broad hand on my shoulder. "Dick, Dick, it not be a suggestion."

All this happened right in front of the nine Africans. I guess Calico Jack didn't think they were smart enough to understand what he was saying to me. But they must have understood plenty, for right then all nine of the Africans ran for the rails and dove over. All but Mark Twain. He hobbled.

"Shoot him!"

I cocked the hammer, but I took my time aiming.

"I meant shoot him now!"

I pointed the pistol's barrel almost directly into the back of the chief.

"Fer gawd's sake, man, kill him!"

Mark Twain had almost reached the railing.

I pulled the trigger.

POW!

The shot sailed high, just as I'd planned.

Calico Jack snatched the pistol from me, cocked its hammer, and aimed directly into the back of the chief, who by this time, was hobbling pretty fast.

The musket ball pinned the white shirt into the blood-soaked cavity it had created. Without hesitating, Calico Jack whipped out a second pistol, aimed, and fired, putting an end to Mark Twain's agonizing screams.

All around us was splashing as the Africans tried to swim away from the trader.

Calico Jack slowly walked over to where the African chief lay and, with his boot, pushed him through the rails. "Sharks 'ill be along shortly ter take care of them others. Now then, let's set about getting this trader fit fer hunting." Pointing at the crimson stain on the deck, he added, "Clean up this mess."

In case you're wondering, right then is when my fascination with pirates ended.

CHAPTER TWENTY FOUR

THE SQUALL BEFORE THE STORM

"Turtles?" Scary Mary said in a not-so-friendly voice.

"And cocoa-nuts?" Anne Bonny asked.

"Conch?" said Grinning George Fetherston who was not grinning so much. "We be eating conch fritters, now?"

"Confound it all, it's the ship that matters, not its cargo."

"No, love, it's the cargo that matters. Leastways to the crew."

"I call for a vote," Scary Mary said.

"On?" said Calico Jack.

"Captain of the *William*," Scary Mary replied. "The men and Anne and me conversed about the matter while you and the boy took possession of this turtle-conch trader. We are all of one accord and that accord be that you're unfit."

"Unfit, am I?"

Heads nodded.

"Mary is right, love. Thus far you have delivered only promises."

"And cocoa-nuts," said Fearless Fenis Fenwick who, at that very moment, was feasting on the chunky, white meat of a freshly hacked-open coconut.

Calico Jack whirled to face the circle of men and two women who had gathered around him. "Fine, but I give you fair warning, Mary. You hain't got the brains of a cockroach when it comes ter hunting a prize. Ter be sure, ye talk a fine lie, ye do. Claims ter sail with conviction and cunning. Ye may strike fear in the hearts of them men who drink and get drunk in yer establishment, but by thunder I'll not quake at yer words, ye may lay to that. A vote it 'tis."

"You lost the *Ranger*," Scary Mary said. "You lost your vessel to them Spaniards back on Isla de Los Pinos. And your men lost your flagship to Woodes Rogers."

I have to say, placing blame on the crew for the loss of Calico Jack's other ship didn't seem like a smart move, but maybe Scary Mary knew more about pirate politics and influencing voters than I gave her credit for.

"Ye done?" said Calico Jack.

"Finally, you stole a vessel from under the nose of the British Royal Navy, which is sure to raise the suspicions of the governor and for what? To take a turtle-conch trader."

"And cocoa-nuts," said Patty Cake Carty, mashing coconut pulp into a cake-like paste.

"Fine. Keep yer blasted crew and ship. Only I keep the boy. He has the plan. He has the route of the *Nuestra Señora de Riqueza*. And he'll lead us ter the treasure ship if you'll allow. Only ye won't allow. So I resign, by thunder! Elect whom you please to be your cap'n now. I'm done with ye." Turning to me Calico Jack said, "Come on, Dick. Let's fetch a gig and take possession of that trader."

"You will not wait for the vote?" Anne Bonny said.

"Seems the crew has struck their colors. Not interested in capturing the *Nuestra Señora de Riqueza*, they be. Care nothing fer the gold and silver and precious stones she carries. Very well, I'll not waste my time leading such a churlish rabble."

"Jack!" one of the crew shouted. "Boss Man forever! Boss Man Jack for cap'n!" A few of the other men joined in, shouting, "JACK, JACK, JACK!!"

"So that's yer tune now, is it? First ye want Mary here ter lead ye, next it be me. Which is it? Make it clear.'

"JACK FOR CAP'N! JACK FOR SKIP!"

At this Calico Jack grinned. "Well now, Mary. I reckon yer 'll have ter wait fer the tide to turn. And now, shipmates, let's be about the business of fashioning this vessel fer hunting."

"I suppose you'll be wanting to cast me adrift in a gig," said Scary Mary.

"Fortunate fer you as I'm not a revengeful man. That was never my way. I'm putting ye in charge of that turtle-conch trader. Them men who aligned themselves with ye, you and them can ship over some cannons and fit her out fer fighting. The rest 'ill remain here with me and Dick on the *William*. Cool heads and steady hands be what we'll need now." Calico Jack raised his voice to address the whole crew. "Best set about it getting our fleet into shipshape. Thar's a treasure in store fer ever man who does his duty. Now to it!"

The crew hurried to let down gigs, but Calico Jack grasped my shoulder and pulled me aside. Whispering in my ear with rum-soaked breath, "Dick, ye seen the lay of things. Them men, they'll not much abide simpletons and dunderheads. They mean to have treasure and soon. Can ye lay a course to that treasure ship? Speak plain, now."

"I'm pretty sure of it, yes."

"Fine, then. 'Cause I must say, ye fail ter find that vessel soon, and it'll be you and me them fellers 'ill feed ter the sharks."

CHAPTER TWENTY FIVE

Scary Mary's Merry Men

Not long after we separated into two vessels, the lookout aboard the *William* spied a rich East Indian ship.

"East Indians be floating gold mines fer pirates," said Calico Jack. "Especially them that be en route to England with their wealthy cargoes from India. Odd ter see one this far west, though."

"What be the orders, sir."

"Send the turtle-conch trader against her. We'll see if them Indians be up fer a fight."

"You sure that is wise?" Anne Bonny said. "If we both attack at once I feel confident she will run up the white flag."

"Or send us both ter Davy Jones. Could be the Indian's crew be up fer a fight and heavily armed, too. Mary wants ter be captain, does she. Let's see what she's made of."

I could spend a great deal of time explaining how the turtle-conch trader maneuvered into position and ran down the East Indian freighter, but by now I'm sure you know how these pirate attacks go. It's always pretty much the same. Which is to say that pirates would rather scare a hapless crew into surrendering than fight it out. Fighting means some pirates might die. Better to bully a crew into giving up if you can.

And that's just what Mary and her merry men attempted to do.

First there was the shot across the bow. This only encouraged the Indians to roll out more canvas, trim sheets, and sail away.

"Confound it all, don' that fool captain know it's pirates chasing him?"

"Could be if you run up your special flag he'd hove to, boss," said Black Eye Patch Baker.

"Fine idea," said Calico Jack.

Up went the skull and crossbones. Except on Calico Jack's special flag he had replaced the crossbones with crossed swords. The flag did not have the result we'd hoped. The East Indians continued sailing away.

"Why don' she blast that freighter out of the water?" said Calico Jack. "What's she waiting fer?"

Right then the East Indian hove to. A cry went up. With eager excitement Calico Jack's men watched as the two vessels drew closer. All the while the *William* remained well out of range of the East Indian's guns. Which, as we were about to discover, turned out to be a good move on Calico Jack's part.

Gunports sprang open on the East Indian ship. As cannon after cannon fired, muzzled flashes erupted in sequences. Balls smashed through the turtle-conch trader rigging. Other ordinances splashed in the water around the smaller pirate vessel. With the Indian's first full broadside she brought down the turtle-conch trader's mainmast. Her second broadside tore into the trader's hull, leaving her rolling and settling in the sea.

"Get her moving," Calico Jack barked. "Fer the love of Lazarus, fall off!"

We all understood his instructions were for Scary Mary, but of course she was well beyond the range of his voice. Besides which, she had her hands full.

As if in answer, a second broadside blasted from the Indians. Several balls struck the trader's rigging, splintering wood, tearing lines.

"Confound it all," said Calico Jack, "get the devil out of there!"

But the turtle-conch trader did not fall off. In fact, she fell over.

The next broadside tore through the turtle-conch trader's hull at the waterline. That precision of the volley would have been something to be admired if not for the fact that Mary and her merry men were the ones being pounded into oblivion.

"She is certainly well-manned," Anne Bonny said. "And trained well."

The final broadside shredded the deck, destroyed the rudder, and riddled the waterline with holes so large they could be seen with the naked eye. At that point the turtle-conch trader began to slip under whitecaps.

"What be yer orders, boss?"

Calico Jack looked about as if unsure.

By now it was obvious to every man on the *William* that we were outgunned and probably outsmarted, captain-wise.

"Shall we launch the gigs to retrieve the survivors?"

"Not likely. Remain here and them Indians will move within range and fire on us. We'll go to Davy Jones same as them on that conch trader."

"But we cannot leave them," Anne Bonny pleaded.

"Ye know the code. One fer all and all fer none when the none be done fer."

The turtle-conch trader slipped under and sank. Those who could, the able-bodied, made use of whatever wood and

THE END OF CALICO JACK

flotsam they could to stay afloat. The wind carried the cries of the wounded across the water.

"Jack, I'll not allow this. We must send the gigs to help."

"And die?"

"If be so, yes. Mary would not abandon you."

"Not more than an hour ago she was ready ter maroon me on an island."

"The boy and I will go," Anne Bonny said.

I gulped. "We will?"

"We will get all the survivors we can and return forthwith. Do not tack away until we have," Anne Bonny said to Calico Jack. "Understood?"

"Be gone already. But be quick about it."

Which is how I ended up in a gig with Anne Bonny as we paddled furiously to save what was left of Scary Mary's merry men.

CHAPTER TWENTY SIX

Hobbling Dobbin Earns His Keep

Let me just say that Calico Jack was not the most popular captain in the West Indies when Mary and her merry men finally climbed back aboard the *William*. I suppose he knew there was a squall brewing—and here I'm talking about the rage of Scary Mary—so our illustrious captain retreated to his cabin with a fresh bottle of rum. There he proceeded to bolt the door shut. For good measure he pushed a dresser in front.

The East Indian freighter had poured on the canvas and fled as soon as we launched our gigs. By the time we had retrieved the survivors and reached the *William*, the Indians were over the horizon and out of sight. The crew that wasn't stabbed, shot, or dying lounged about.

"Coward." Scary Mary spat the word. "Standing off and refusing to engage. Less than a coward. A coward's coward." To me she said, "Where be this surgeon you found?"

THE END OF CALICO JACK

To be honest, I had no idea where Hobbling Dobbin was. I hadn't laid eyes on Hobbling Dobbin since we stowed aboard after stealing the *William*. But off I went to look … and found him in an infinitesimally minute cabin. Basically, he was napping in a broom closet. He had tossed the wooden buckets and deck mops into the hallway. For a bed, he had crammed a mattress into the closet.

"For breakfast," Hobbling Dobbin said, "I had bacon, scrambled eggs, a strawberry waffle, mixed fruit, cinnamon applesauce, and a slice of cantaloupe with coffee."

He seemed quite pleased with the report of his diet pyramid. "You had all that for breakfast?" I asked. "On this ship?"

"Mind over matter, mate. It don't matter what you eat if you have a mind for imagination."

"You're needed on deck. We have wounded."

"Of what sort?"

"Of the bleeding and dying sort. Bring your doctor's bag."

Here's the good news. Hobbling Dobbin actually turned out to be a half-decent doctor. Using sail needles and thread he stitched flesh. With a hammer he broke, then reset a few bones. With a carpenter's saw he shortened a few legs and arms.

But he couldn't save the most severely wounded and the crew was none too happy about that. I understood why they were angry. The general opinion was that, had we attacked with both ships, we might have taken the freighter and lost less men and the men who survived, lost less limbs. I seriously doubt it would have mattered. The East Indian ship was vastly larger and better armed than we were. But I kept my mouth shut. It seemed like the smart move.

Two crewmembers brought another of the wounded to Hobbling Dobbin. The deck before me was a bloody mess. All around us lay fingers and limbs and at least one foot.

Hobbling Dobbin said to his current patient, "You can survive this, man, but you'll need the will to want."

"Can't, doc. I'm done fer."

"You have the strength, you must try."

For a few moments the poor man lay there without breathing. A bloody shirt covered his face and forehead. Only his lips showed. The man went so long without moving that I thought he had died. Then after, like, twenty seconds, he gasped for air.

"Be brave, man." Hobbling Dobbin lifted the bloody shirt to attend to the cuts on the patient's cheek and nose.

The man's face was so covered with blood and his bangs so matted that it took me a moment to recognize him: One-Tooth Tommy Earl. He was the crew closest to my age. Had he lived in our neighborhood back in Quiet Cove we would have been in high school together. That's how young he was.

Through clinched teeth One-Tooth Tommy Earl wheezed, "She was beautiful."

"Your girlfriend?" Hobbling Dobbin applied a tourniquet to One-Tooth Tommy Earl's mangled arm.

"Daughter." He struggled to breathe, the lifting and falling of his chest slowed. "Tabatha …"

I would have thought him too young to be a dad, but if he'd run off as a boy, which I knew from my reading many boys did during pirate times, he would have become a man at a young age.

"Save your strength," said Hobbling Dobbin. "You'll need it later for when you recover."

"Do not regret …" His voice became a weak wheeze … "signing on as crew." One-Tooth Tommy Earl's eyes clouded.

Hobbling Dobbin dipped a bloody rag in a bucket of seawater and pressed it into a gapping hole in One-Tooth Tommy Earl's chest.

I expected One-Tooth Tommy Earl to flinch. I would have. Instead his glassy eyes stared upwards at the sky.

"But I'll miss …" A single tear left a silver trail on his leather-brown cheek. "Tabatha. No doubt she'll …"

His head tipped slightly to one side. A raspy whistle escaped from his throat. Though One-Tooth Tommy Earl's eyes remained opened, his chest moved no more.

Hobbling Dobbin went about the business of rinsing his tool and wiping blood off his hands. Then he barked: "Next!"

And on it went for the remainder of the afternoon.

By nightfall all the wounded had been moved below into the galley where they could be attended. The dead were shipped over the side with little ceremony, which only attracted more sharks. The mood aboard the *William* was not what you would call upbeat and cheerful.

"You have to tell him," Anne Bonny said to me.

"Yes," seconded Scary Mary. "It's best if it comes from you."

The two women had found me at the back of the *William*, watching our white wake disappear into blackness.

"Me tell who what?"

"The crew is spent," Anne Bonny said. "They want to turn back." She handed me a scribbled note. "It's their verdict. Slip it under Jack's door."

I stared at the scrap of paper. "Why me?"

"Because all this was your plan. You talked him into it."

I almost replied that it *wasn't* my plan and I hadn't talked anyone into doing anything, but arguing with two cold-blooded female pirates packing swords, dirks, and flintlock pistols didn't seem like a smart move.

"Maybe our luck will change," I said hopefully.

"Not with Jack as captain, it won't," said Scary Mary. "The only luck he has is the bad kind."

I trudged off to deliver the news. And knocked and knocked and …

"Confound it all! Can't a body get a bit of rest?"

From the other side of the door I heard grunting, furniture scraping across hardwood. Before he could open the door, I added, "The crew has called a meeting on deck. I'll tell them you're on the way."

If you're thinking I should have slipped the piece of paper under his door and told Calico Jack that he'd been voted out as captain, I get that. But the thing is, I was afraid. I could tell from the banging and cursing and glass breaking that he was in no mood for a calm conversation about his future as captain or legacy as a famous pirate. I was honestly afraid that if I said such a thing, he would have pulled a pistol and shot me through the door. There had been lots of ways the voyage could have gone wrong and we seemed to be checking each and every one.

"See here," said Calico Jack, staggering up the short flight of steps that led to the aft (back) of the ship. "Has old Jack ever missed his mark?"

Crew: "YES!"

"Have I ever tucked tail and run?"

Crew: "YES!"

This retort had to hurt since Calico Jack had charged his former mentor, Charles Vane, of cowardness. It was the reason he'd become captain of the *Ranger*.

"Have I ever lost a man?"

"YES!"

"I meant men I liked."

This seemed to quiet the crew for a moment. I think maybe each man was wondering if Calico Jack liked him.

"You've lost half your fleet," said Scary Mary, "half the men on half your fleet, and all the treasure that was on that East Indian."

"She has a point, love," echoed Anne Bonny. "We've talked it over with the crew. All agree that a change in leadership is best."

"What say you, Dick? Ye throwing yer lot in with this rabble?"

"I … ah … think, ah …" I continued staring at the horizon, refusing to look at the captain or crew or the two women. In the distance, barely visible, I spied the faint silhouette of a dark shape. "… that there's a ship out there."

Calico Jack rushed to my side, looked to where I pointed, and yelled, "Where be the lookout who's supposed ter look out fer ships?"

"Here, boss." Black Eye Patch Baker raised his hand. "The women said the crew was holding a vote. I didn't want to be left out. Every vote counts, you know."

"Confound it all," said Calico Jack. He placed the spyglass to his eye. "British fer sure."

"Has she spotted us?" said Scary Mary.

"More'n likely," replied Calico Jack. "No doubt *they* have a lookout."

This was an obvious dig at the two ladies and crew.

"While the two of ye were scheming ter take over command ye led us inter a trap. Bend your backs, lads, and trim the sails!"

"But what about the vote?" asked Black Eye Patch Baker.

"Yes, love. There is the matter of the vote."

"Confound it all, the vote be delayed. That be the pirate code. No change in captain during battle."

"But we are not engaged in battle," Anne Bonny said.

"Will be soon enough. Now not be the time ter change captains. 'Sides, I daresay by sunup we'll fetch upon the *Nuestra de Whatever*, hain't that right, Dick?"

"Um?"

"I say, hain't that right, Dick?"

"Yes sir!"

And just like that I made a promise before the whole crew that we would escape the British warship and find a Spanish treasure ship, all before breakfast.

Some days I'm such an idiot.

CHAPTER TWENTY SEVEN

THE STORM BEFORE THE STORM

I wish I could say we escaped, but when dawn broke it was clear the British warship had closed the gap between us. No doubt the British ship had more men to trim the sails and a more competent skipper. All we had were a skeleton crew of tired, hungry, and complaining pirates.

Which was actually the good news.

Thomas B. Quick climbed down from his perch in the crow's nest to deliver the bad news in person. "Got some bad news, boss," said the lookout.

"It's a new day, mate," said Calico Jack. "A fresh start. Let's not ruin it, shall we?"

"Aye, aye, boss. Only thing is, and I wouldn't dare bring this up unless it were something of deadly importance, there be a warship off our bow."

"You mean stern."

THE END OF CALICO JACK

"Stern, yes, but look there ahead." Thomas B. Quick pointed in front of us across dreary, gray water.

I could see nothing but whitecaps and a large, low band of black clouds spewing tendrils of rain, which, of course, we were sailing right into. Out came Calico Jack's spyglass. He scanned the horizon in front of the *William*, mumbled a string of bad words, then proceeded to make a slow three-sixty turn.

"Confound it all, look out there." Calico Jack passed Anne Bonny the spyglass. "It's that Spanish warship what hunted us down and stole our sloop."

"But, love," Anne Bonny countered, "was us that took *their* sloop, first."

"Well *somebody* stole *some* sloop and now they've tracked us down, again. How's that possible?" Calico Jack whirled and pointed a gnarled, crooked finger at me. "This is all your fault. Ye'll get forty lashes fer this. Was yer idea to steal the sloop in the first place. And yer idea to leave that bounty hunter behind on the sloop."

I kept quiet. Not because it seemed like the smart move—which of course it was. Never argue with a pirate. Or the captain. Or, and this I learned last semester, your teacher. But because all my focus was on the flash of lightning in the approaching thunderstorm and the roiling clouds that looked as if any moment they might form a waterspout.

"Don't go blaming the boy," Anne Bonny said. "It's not all his fault." She looked as if she might say more, hesitated, and looked me up and down with a disapproving frown. "But I will allow that if not for him we might not be in this mess."

"If you had not renounced our deal and run off to join Jack and Anne, we would not be in this predicament," said Scary Mary to me.

"See? Told you it was yer fault," said Calico Jack. I half-expected him to stick out his tongue at me.

"Tie him to the mast. Give him the lash! Keelhaul him!"

"Way ahead of you," said Calico Jack. "But right now we need to direct our fire at that British man-of-war behind us." He pointed astern. "Closing fast, she is, and right up our bumhole. She'll blast us to kingdom come."

"If the Spanish do not blast us out of the water first," Anne Bonny said.

Calico Jack spun and got right in my face. "What's the plan, Dick?"

Given that toothpaste, mouthwash, and breath mints were in short supply on the *William*, I was sort of thinking that forty lashes with a whip might not be the worst thing in the world.

I replied, "I thought you didn't like my plans."

"Like 'em fine 'till they don' work."

"Come on," Anne Bonny said to me. "You must have some thoughts on how we can escape this mess."

"And whatever your thoughts," said Scary Mary, "they better be good ones."

"Ah, Skip, we got another problem," said Edward Bilge Swill Warner.

"Not now. I'm in the middle of a planning session."

"But it's mightily important."

"Like this not be?"

"Has to do with a warship, Skip."

"I know, I know," said Calico Jack. "Which is why I need ye ter pipe down. I can only deal with two warship problems at a time."

"Then ye'll not like this problem."

At that all four of us looked at Edward Bilge Swill Warner who did, in fact, look and smell as if he'd been dipped from head to toe in the rank water that sloshed about at the bottom of the *William*.

I'm sure I do not need to tell you that he was pointing at the horizon, only not at the British man-of-war or the Spanish warship.

THE END OF CALICO JACK

"Don' tell me that's the …" said Calico Jack, his words trailing off.

"East Indian freighter, yes, Skip. And from the looks of her, she means business."

"Notify the gun crews," said Calico Jack. "The signals will be: ready to fire, one, two, three, fire. Got it?"

"Aye, aye, Skip."

"Plan, Dick. We need a plan! And we need it now!"

"Yes, what is the plan?" Anne Bonny asked.

"Forty lashes is my vote," said Scary Mary.

Looking about the *William*, then at the East Indian freighter that was bearing down on us, back at the British man-of-war, and finally at the Spanish warship, I told them my plan.

"It will never work," Scary Mary said.

Anne Bonny replied, "It might."

"It better. Else there be the devil ter pay," added Calico Jack. "And this devil be having pimples on his back that need popping."

Of all the plans I'd suggested, I felt least confident about that one.

Which, of course meant it was only a matter of minutes before I would be popping pimples on our captain's back. That's if I survived my lashing at the mast. Some days it doesn't pay to be a pirate.

CHAPTER TWENTY EIGHT

THE MAELSTROM STORM

The Spanish warship bow cannon spit fire. I saw it: then I heard it. A small shot whistled through the air.

"Hot as a mule in heat," said Calico Jack, shaking his fist in the air.

A second volley splintered wood on the poop deck, but did little damage.

"Order your men to hold fire," I said. "Let her get closer."

"Let her get closer?" said Scary Mary. "Tell me how we could do other? She'll run us down if we do not reply with a blast."

"Keep your wits," said Calico Jack. "Dick's plan may yet work."

Directly ahead the bow of the Spanish warship plunged into the sea and each time she drove down, a huge, white parting wake erupted from her gleaming black hull. Behind us, farther back but not that much, the British warship had rolled out its bow cannons. It was obvious to all on deck that at any moment she too would swing broadside and hurl her hellish shells at us. To the east the East Indian freighter, with her treasure-laden cargo, sailed right for us.

"Uh-oh," I said.

"Uh-oh, what?" Anne Bonny said.

"Look!" Everyone looked to where I pointed. And where I pointed wasn't at any of the three ships. I pointed up where the spinning, spiraling, tendril of a huge waterspout began to descend from the biggest, ugliest black cloud I'd ever seen. "Drop the anchor! DO IT NOW!"

Even now I can't believe the crew listened to me. I mean, it wasn't like I held any real authority over the three famous pirates. But without any argument at all the crew deployed the bow anchor, then the stern. Anne Bonny yelled for the crew to brace themselves.

The *William* wrenched, rolled, groaned, turned, and for a few terrifying moments actually buried its leeward rail in the water. Then she righted herself and shuddered. At that very moment a horrific BOOM exploded from behind. A second BOOM followed quickly, from ahead of us and off to one side. Then a third, not as close or loud, echoed as the East Indians unleashed a volley at us. Right then is when my great plan almost proved to be our undoing.

The maelstrom struck with furious intensity. Black clouds split, crackled with lightning, and unleashed a torrential downpour that fell so fast and so hard that I lost sight of both ends of the *William*. Within moments, the wind was screaming through the rigging with gale-force strength, lashing us with stinging pellets of rain. The seas increased from small waves to mountains of water that tossed the *William* onto her port rail. Each man knew that this was just the beginning. The wind, and the rain, and the seas seemed to swallow us, and no doubt would as soon as the waterspout moved over the *William*.

"The anchors!" I yelled. "We'll sink if we do not get free. Cut the anchors."

"But ye just said we was to deploy them," yelled Calico Jack over the shrieking howls of the wind.

"And now I'm saying we need to cut loose."

Moving quickly, the crew cut the cables.

"The oars!" I yelled. "We need to get moving!"

"MAN THE OARS!" yelled Calico Jack. Instantly oars were deployed through cannon ports. "Bend yer backs into it, lads!"

The crew sprang to work with an energy that reflected the fear we all felt. While most pulled the oars, others cleared the decks of shredded canvas. A smaller group fought to get a sail over the side, and plug the holes below the waterline where cannon balls had found their mark. Grunts and cursing could be heard above the shrieking wind as the men worked on slippery, wet decks, each knowing that at the next instant he might be swept overboard, and that no one would even see it happen.

Since it was my plan, Calico Jack ordered me to the bowsprit with instructions to guide us out of the storm, out of range of the three ships, and to safety.

I did not like our chances of doing any of this, but I kept my reservations to myself.

Right then the ghostly shape of the Spanish warship passed by our starboard side, coming so close I could have hit her with a dirk dart. But here's the scary part. Jack Sparrow stood on the bowsprit, shaking his fist at me and yelling some words that, while I could not hear them due to the booming thunder and howling wind, did not seem to be those of a welcoming greeting.

The Spanish warship sailed straight into the space we had vacated. At that instant a cacophonous crashing volley of fire erupted from amidst the storm's thick grayness. The thunderous broadside came so close it shook the deck of the *William*. In reply from the opposite side of the *William* another volley erupted. Pounding rain and lashing wind slung sea spray across our decks. I could not see the shape of any of the vessels. I only knew that had we remained anchored where we had been, the *William* would have been blown to bits. The storm screamed with demonic fury. The deck beneath my feet creaked and groaned in long, agonizing moans. Then came the terrifying howl of a train's horn.

The waterspout was upon us.

Wind slammed into the *William* with the shockwave force of a nuclear explosion. (Not really, but it seemed like it.) The *William* rolled onto her side. Waves slammed perpendicular into our deck. Men clung to whatever they could grab to keep from getting swept over. This all happened in like ten seconds. Then the screaming wind and rain passed and the *William* righted herself. Water poured over the sides and back into the sea.

From off our stern, hidden by the whirling vortex, came a terrible wood-crunching, mast-snapping collision. The deadly, spinning waterspout spit out bits of ship, sails, and a few bodies. By the time we sailed into misty rain and the wind lessened, all that remained of the three warships was a smear of wreckage on the gray sea.

We had escaped.

Which also meant that I was something of a hero.

But as I'm sure you guessed, that did not last long.

CHAPTER TWENTY NINE

I Walk The Plank

"Where be this *Nuestra de Whatever*?" said Calico Jack. The two of us stood far away from the huddled clot of men and two women who had gathered near the back of the *William*. It was clear the women and crew were up to something, and I had a hunch it was the vote to replace Calico Jack as captain. Which meant I would most likely be voted off the ship too.

"Let's go to your cabin," I said. "I'll show you on the chart where the treasure ship should be."

In the captain's cabin he unrolled the chart as before and anchored the four corners with his flintlock pistol, dirk, cutlass, and a lit candle. "Tell me plain, can ye find her?"

I studied the chart, examining the squares indicating longitude and latitude. When I found the right square I thumped my finger on a spot due west of the southwest corner of a large island. "There. The *Nuestra Señora de Riqueza* will be there this morning on a course sailing due north through the passage between Hispaniola and Cuba." Without looking up I asked, "Where are we?"

He pulled out a pocket watch and smiled. "Unless I miss my mark, we be there." He tapped the square directly north of where I had indicated the *Nuestra Señora de Riqueza* should be.

"So we're close."

"If you say so. Thing is, Dick, you could be lying. Pirates be known ter lie a bit."

"I'm not a pirate."

"Ye dress like a pirate. Ye smell like a pirate. And ye ne'er did say how it was ye came ter fetch up on Isla del Hombre Cabra."

"You never asked."

"This be me asking, now."

Bending over the chart I found the tiny spec that was Coffin Cay. "There," I said, pointing at a dot no bigger than a pinhead. "That's where I was right before I arrived on Goat Man Island."

"You sailed from there to Isla del Hombre Cabra?"

Trying to explain how I had an epileptic episode and mysteriously showed up off Goat Man Island without any recollection of sailing there seemed like something that was best left unspoken, so I said, "Post lookouts. Alert the crew. If I'm right, we'll sight the treasure ship by noon."

"Assuming there still *be* a crew."

There came a knock on the cabin door. "Your presence is requested on deck, sir."

"Who be that darkening my door?"

"Little John Davis."

"And Little Elton John Eaton."

"And Little John Cole."

Calico Jack leaned across the map toward me and said quietly, "Crappy little crew, them three Little Johns."

"Not funny, boss!"

"Very well, inform the crew I'll be there forthwith."

"And bring the lad," said one of the Little Johns. The heavy clumping of their footsteps retreated.

Calico Jack rolled up the chart and strapped on his cutlass, dirk, and pistol. "Well, Dick? We're in fer it now. It'll be a gig fer the two of us. Or maybe jest fer me."

"But what about the *Nuestra Señora de Riqueza*?"

"Pirates not be known fer having much in the way of patience. I can tell 'em we're 'bout to come upon the prize, but I doubt it'll matter. My oaths be not carrying water like they did. Ter many close calls and missed prizes."

The crew of the *William* met us on deck.

"Love," Anne Bonny said, "understand this was not how I wanted things to end."

"I did," said Scary Mary. "This is how I hoped it would end. I knew from the start that you were a lying, thieving, backstabbing, good-fer-nothing captain."

"Is that it?" said Calico Jack, snatching the scrap from Scary Mary's hand. "That be the verdict?" He unfolded the crumpled paper, grunted, and passed it to me.

I tallied the votes. Calico Jack had one in his favor. I assumed it was Anne Bonny.

"Well, let's be done with this," he said. "Do we get a gig?"

Anne Bonny shook her head. "Sorry, love. The crew feels we may need them later should we come upon trouble."

"Or a prize," said Scary Mary.

"Ye expect us ter swim?"

"A plank a piece for floating should suffice," said Scary Mary.

Big John Howard tossed over a not-in-great-shape deck plank.

Scary Mary unsheathed her sword and poked Calico Jack in the back. "Off ye go."

Without hesitating, Calico Jack jumped in after his plank.

"I had nothing to do with this," I pleaded. "I was only obeying orders."

"First off," said Scary Mary, "you defaulted on the terms of our agreement made in my office, and you ran off. Second, you sided with Calico Jack when it came to the matter of who was most fit to be captain. Third, I don't care." She jabbed me not so gently in the back with her dirk. "You struck your colors. Now you'll live with your choice."

Big John Hanson tossed over a second plank. I inhaled deeply and jumped in. Resting my chest on the plank, I kicked hard to catch up with Calico Jack. This took some doing since he had a head start, plus, the *William* continued to sail along briskly.

When at last I did reach him, I said, "Is this what pirates call 'walking the plank?'"

"Ne'er heard it put that way, but when ye say it like that … yes, yes it—"

"SAIL HO!"

We both looked back up at the crew gathered along the rail. "Sail?" I said.

"THERE!" One of the men pointed at the square canvas coming over the horizon from the south.

"Can't be." I squinted against the glare of the sun's light reflecting off the water.

"It be," said Calico Jack. "Mark my word, that be a merchant vessel and a large one."

"You know what this means?"

"That your plan worked?" said Calico Jack.

"That my plan worked."

I must admit; I was the most surprised of any of us.

CHAPTER THIRTY

THE PRIZE

Minutes later we were fished back aboard the *William*. "I suppose once we take that vessel ye'll be tossing us both over again."

"NO!" shouted the crew in unison. "JACK BE OUR CAP'N! JACK! BE BOSS MAN FOREVER!"

"There's been a change in leadership during your very brief absence," Anne Bonny continued. "Mary is no longer the captain."

"How come?"

"Let's just say the crew did not particularly like her management style. She's below in the brig stewing."

Men lined the quarterdeck (the part of the upper deck behind the mainmast), poop deck (the area behind the mizzenmast aft and atop the cabin roof), and forecastle (the upper deck forward of the front mast), awaiting their assignments. High aloft standing on the spreaders I saw a small band of men move quickly into position.

"How come you don't have archers in the crow's nest?" I asked. "That way they can shoot burning arrows into the sails of the *Nuestra Señora de Riqueza*."

Anne Bonny eyed the upper half of the mast. "Jack? Do you have archers?"

"Do I have archers? What sort of captain of a pirate ship would I be if I didn't have archers?" Turning to Patty Cake Carty, Calico Jack said in a hushed voice, "Rustle up some men with bows and arrows put them in the crew's nest."

"You mean crow's nest," said Patty Cake Carty, correcting him.

"And make sure they bring some arrows with them. Last time them useless fellers looked like a choir of angels up there strumming one-string harps."

Fearless Fenis Fenwick approached our small clot. "Men are all fitted out and at their quarters, Cap'n. Where do you want the lad?"

"Bowsprit 'ill do nicely." Calico Jack pointed toward a short platform jutting off the bow. "Dick be the one who brought us ter the *Nuestra de Whatever*. So it'll be him that lays eyes on her first." To Black Eye Patch Baker he said, "Most likely the captain 'ill make a run fer it. See to it we have enough black eye patches in case some of the crew loses an eye or whatever."

"Aye, aye, cap'n."

"Aye, aye, cap'n," chuckled Calico Jack. "That Black Eye Patch Baker cracks me up."

I stood alone on the bowsprit, clinging to ropes and railings for balance. That far forward with the heaving sea directly below me was like trying to stand in a roller coaster car. One misstep and I'd fall into the waves and be crushed beneath the hull. From amidships came a call from Calico Jack. "Guns be ready?"

"Aye, cap'n," Fearless Fenis Fenwick said. "Double-shotted, as ordered, sir."

Lowering his spyglass Calico Jack called, "In that case run up the colors! We'll see how the rabbit runs when the fox is on her heels."

The flag had barely reached the top of the mast before cheers and howls went up among the crew. I admit, a rush of excitement swept over me. Pirating was not in my blood. I detested everything about it. But the idea of capturing a ship did make my heart pound with excitement. With her sails snapping taut, the *William* surged forward. Even without a spyglass I could see the *Nuestra Señora de Riqueza* crew hurrying into position.

"How's she rigged?" called Calico Jack. "For fight or to flee?"

"She's turnin' off, sir," replied Fearless Fenis Fenwick. "And tryin' to run."

"Ready about! Hard alee!" Calico Jack's voice boomed over the rattle of sails and rush of water.

The *William's* bow pivoted smartly; we gave chase. We had the wind of her; we had a straight shot at the vessel, and we were gaining quickly.

"She's within range, sir," called Fearless Fenis Fenwick.

"Ready the long guns! We'll strike a blow and see if she'll run up the white flag."

The words had no more left his mouth when a shot whistled past my head. It slammed into one of the lower spreaders, snapping it off. Thomas Bourn Brown tumbled from the rigging and crashed onto the deck. Withering in pain, he clutched the nub of what remained of his leg, blood spurting through his fingers.

"DICK! Ye be in charge of warning us when she lets fly!"

From the stern of the *Nuestra Señora de Riqueza* came a second puff of smoke.

"INCOMING!" I shouted.

THE END OF CALICO JACK

The cannon shot came in lower this time and splintered wood in the aft castle.

"By thunder we'll kill 'em all, every last one of them! Let fire the guns!"

The bowsprit shuddered beneath me. In the distance I saw the explosion take down the *Nuestra Señora de Riqueza*'s mast and sails and left her listing severely. A cry of "JACK, JACK, JACK!" went up from the crew. Another volley from the *William* and a white flag rose and fluttered above the *Nuestra Señora de Riqueza*.

The crew jumped and shouted and cheered at the sight: sort of like fans do at a ball game when someone hits a home run or makes a game-winning jump shot. But I did not join them. I knew what was to come. Killing and butchering, and I wanted no part of it.

CHAPTER THIRTY ONE

Nuestra Señora de Riqueza

Jack took no pity on the crew of the *Nuestra Señora de Riqueza*.

One man was pinned to the foremast. The boatswain was crucified where he stood: nailed in place with spikes driven through his feet into the deck. The remaining crew was blindfolded and kicked into a kneeling position. Men were arranged in line like dominos. While one of the pirates held terrified men in place at the point of a cutlass, the other fired a small cannon brought over from the *William*. With one volley a hole was blasted through the crewmembers' midsections and they fell like dominos.

The most horrific torture was saved for the captain of the *Nuestra Señora de Riqueza*. Threatening to reduce the poor man's fingers one digit at a time, Calico Jack demanded he be told where the treasure was stored. The captain refused. Calico

THE END OF CALICO JACK

Jack repeated his question, pounding the man to the deck. The captain was still shaking his head when Richard Corner Pocket whipped out a dirk and cut off the man's thumb. The captain's shrieking cries only brought laughter to the pirates. Little John Cole lopped off the man's forefinger. Little John Davis ... the middle finger. Little John Eaton ... the pinky. And so it went until the poor captain's hands were bloody nubs.

That's when Big Ben Palmer stretched the captain's arm over the rim of an open hatch. Without waiting for Calico Jack's orders, Scary Mary Read swung her cutlass, chopping off the arm at the elbow.

For years I had read pirate books and watched pirate movies and secretly admired pirates for their adventurous bravery and lust for freedom and treasure. No more. Now the word *pirate* no longer meant swashbuckling hero. Forever more I would see pirates as gang-like thugs, terrorists, and marauding murders.

Calico Jack asked the captain a final time.

Between sobbing screams, he told Calico Jack where the treasure was stored. And what a treasure it was. Opals, sapphires, and bloodstones big as hens' eggs. Great emeralds, gleaming with a clear green light. Bags of gold and bars of silver too numerous to count. Rubies great and small. Candlesticks and porringers, and diamonds so perfect any bride would have been envious.

The treasure was as I'd seen it in the cave and more than I remembered.

All of it was shipped over to the *William* and kept under lock and key. While Calico Jack's men swabbed the *Nuestra Señora de Riqueza's* deck with pitch and turpentine, he, Mary Read, and Anne Bonny blindfolded the helpless crew. Then the three went about with torches and set the deck and ship afire.

I wish I could say the three of them hurried quickly from the burning vessel and into the gigs waiting to take them back to the *William*, but that would be a lie. They seemed to relish the moment. Revel in it, actually. If ever there was any doubt in my mind of the evil that lay in their hearts, it vanished as I watched the crew of the freighter burned alive on deck.

Calico Jack and the two women were cold-blooded murderers—as was their crew.

But it was me who had led them to the *Nuestra Señora de Riqueza*.

Which made me most guilty of all.

CHAPTER THIRTY TWO

THE TREASURE CAVE

As soon as we were back aboard the *William*, Calico Jack distributed the treasure to the crew. His share was stored in two not-so-small storage trunks. While the rest of the crew wandered off to count their take, Calico Jack slipped me a skeleton key. No kidding, it was a real skeleton key.

"What's this to?"
"Yer treasure chest."
"I get my very own treasure chest?"
He nodded. "Since it be ye who found the *Nuestra Señora de Riqueza* it's only fair ye get half as much as me. Only right now I have ter place ye in the brig."
"Wait, what?"
"Mary and Anne don' trust ye. With women trust be a hard thing ter earn."

So with my very own treasure chest skeleton key tucked in my soggy and dirty cargo shorts pocket, off I went to the brig. There I joined three survivors of the *Nuestra Señora de Riqueza*. The trio had promised allegiance to Calico Jack. But like me, Anne Bonny and Scary Mary didn't trust them. Wanted them keel-hauled, in fact. So there I was, confined to the brig with the three survivors, none of us confident that we'd see another day. Now that I'd found the treasure ship there was no need to keep me alive.

Late in the day we dropped anchor in a small cove ringed with palms. Cattle and pigs roamed about on the beach. The crew promptly killed the livestock, of course. By late afternoon a full-fledged beach barbeque had broken out. From all appearances, a raucous evening of eating and drinking and celebrating lay ahead. The four of us in the brig could see all this through a slit in the hull's planks.

It was at that point the pirate called Noah Hardwood came to the brig to inform me that the captain requested my presence on deck.

"Dick, we've work to do," Calico Jack explained.

"What sort of work?"

"Hard work. Tiresome work. The Devil's work." He gestured for me to walk with him to the stern of the ship, so we could speak privately. "Now that the fellers have their share of the loot, they be in ripe spirits. Found a good stash of rum in the captain's cabin, I did, and doled it out generously. Soon as it's dark they'll be shouting and stabbing and shooting as first one, then another, goes off to hide his stash or take another's. That's how come some of the fellers swam back 'fore nightfall. They aim to guard their share. In fine spirits, they are. Too fine, if ye ask me. Soon they'll be passed out on the beach or deck. That'll be when we make our move."

"What move? What are you talking about?"

"You and me, we'll pile our share of the treasure into a gig and row ashore. I already scouted out a nice little hidey hole that'll do nicely. But it'll be our little secret, yours and mine. None of the rest of the crew can know."

I should mention here that my share of the haul from the *Nuestra Señora de Riqueza* amounted to a few Spanish coins, three rubies, and some emeralds. Hardly half as much as Calico Jack's take and certainly not enough to warrant a treasure chest. I shoved my small stash into the pockets of my shorts.

"You're not even going to tell the women?" I said.

"Especially not them. Turned on me, they did, by making Mary captain. Mum's the word."

I had another word for what Calico Jack planned to do and it was not *mum*. *Steal*: that was the word that came to mind. If Calico Jack needed my help hiding his treasure, then it meant he'd kept more than his share. A lot more.

When things quieted down on the beach, we placed two treasure chests in a gig. *Not one but two!* Then we rowed ashore to a spot up a creek he had selected. I couldn't imagine how he'd swindled the crew so easily, but he had, for there was no denying that he'd taken much more of the treasure than was rightfully his—and probably from Scary Mary.

After tromping a good way through a marshy area we came to another smaller, isolated, crescent-shaped beach. The moon was up out of the east and shining brilliantly on the water in the small cove. Beyond, breakers snapped and broke on a reef. In an instant I recognized the cove, the beach, the anchorage: Coffin Cay.

Straight ahead was the cliff riddled with caves that I'd shown my parents. Trees and thickets grew right down to the tide line just as I'd remembered the first time. Perched atop the rim of the cliff was a tree full of green leaves. With Mom and Dad, the beach and cliff had seemed different somehow, when we'd arrived. Now, though, the scene was almost exactly as it had been the night I'd sat on the ledge of the cave with William Shakespeare and talked of living and dying and heaven and hell.

"How we'll get up ter that cave I have no idea," said Calico Jack, "but we will. Mark my word, we will or die trying."

"There's a goat path to the left of the cliff that circles up around back. We'll have to carry the chest one at a time, but it's doable."

"How the devil could you know that?"

"I've been here before. A long time ago. And again not so long ago." I appraised the sheer face of the cliff, remembering how, when the tide came in, the water rushed all the way in and crashed against the base. "We'll need block and tackle and a sturdy rope. That we'll use to secure each chest and lower it down. One of us will be on the ledge to receive, the other to feed it down."

"By thunder ye say it as if ye have done this a time or two."

I did not dare explain why I knew how to lower the chests into the cave—or what would happen after the treasure was secured inside.

We went to work, each of us holding a handle on one end of the chest, and lugging it through underbrush and up the old goat path that circled around the back of the cliff.

Once we reached the summit, Calico Jack looked over at the stub ledge far below us. "Down there ye say?"

"Lower it to the ledge and pull it in. But we'll need rope and stuff. I'll stay here with the two chests while you go back and get what we need."

"And take both chests? No, it'll be ye that goes back ter the ship."

"You know good and well I can't carry either of these two chests all by myself. And were I to try and drag one of them, you'd easily follow the trail. The men won't suspect anything if you go back to the ship, but if I return there will be no end to the questions. They're just as likely to sail off without you."

"Smart as paint ye are, Dick. I seen that the first time I laid eyes on ye." He turned and headed back down the trail.

I can tell you this because you're obviously not going to share what I'm about to say, but I knew what Calico Jack would do. He would go back, get the block and tackle, check on the passed-out crew, and bring back one more of his crew: a fellow named Trembles. The man's name was due to the fact that he had "the shakes," a condition that came from being a drunk—which, among Calico Jack's crew, could have been any one of them. All this I had learned during my episode back at Christmas.

Turned out it was Edward Bilge Swill Warner. As soon as I saw Bilge Swill accompanying the captain I made the connection. Bilge Swill was a not-so-nice way of saying "not-so-great rum," which meant Bilge Swill was not just a pirate but *the pirate* with the "shakes" Turtle Bill had mentioned.

By way of an explanation Calico Jack said, "Needed help carrying stuff." As if lugging block and tackle and rope up a goat path was too difficult for one man. Though in the case of Calico Jack that was probably true.

Edward Bilge Swill Warner tied the rope fast to the storm-twisted tree that grew out over the edge of the cliff. Even though its green leaves shimmered wet in the night air, I knew in but a few years this tree would be withered and nearly dead, its branches bare. While Bilge Swill tied himself into the rope and began scaling down the cliff, I helped Calico Jack secure the first chest with rope to make sure it did not spill open. Once Bilge Swill was on the ledge, we lowered the chest. The man struggled with its weight to get it off the ledge and into the cave, but in a few minutes he appeared again below us. Once we'd lowered the second chest, Calico Jack climbed down the rope to help Bilge Swill drag them back into the cave and

THE END OF CALICO JACK

out of sight of any who might scan the cave's entrance with a spyglass.

I made my way to a place I'd spied earlier where the trail cut through a giant tumble of rock in a zigzag pattern. Under a protruding section of the largest boulder, I hollowed out a hole about a foot deep. Then I placed my small stash of coins and jewels in the hole and covered it over, packing down the dirt, when the sudden gunshot confirmed my worst fears.

I raced back to the summit, arriving just as Calico Jack jerked on the rope. Quickly I pulled him up.

"What happened?" I asked. I knew the answer, of course. Bilge Swill was dead.

"Dreadful business, securing a treasure," he said. "Most always costs some poor soul his life." He brushed dirt off his trousers, paying no attention to the splatter of blood on his shirt.

By the time the sun broke over the horizon we were back aboard. Calico Jack ordered the crew to weigh anchor and the *William* sailed away with a sullen and hungover crew. Only two people knew of the location of the *Nuestra Señora de Riqueza* treasure: me and Calico Jack. Three if you count Bilge Swill."

But as pirates are fond of saying: dead men tell no tales.

CHAPTER THIRTY THREE

CAPTAIN JONATHAN BARNETT

As you might have guessed, I was in a not-so-great mood when I returned to the *William*. The massacre on the *Nuestra Señora de Riqueza* had left me depressed, as had Calico Jack's cold-blooded murder of Edward Bilge Swill Warner. Curling into a ball in a corner of my wet, stinking cell—which was really only a livestock stall with some rotten hay sloshing about—I tried to sleep.

Some hours later I was jolted awake by the sound of cannon fire. Frantic footsteps could be heard running on deck. Loud yelling followed and then more cannon and musket fire. This went on for several minutes before there was a hard "crunch" followed by rattling, which I took to be the grappling hooks. Through my slit in the hull's plank I saw that we had pulled alongside a trading sloop. For several minutes there was yelling and shooting and at least one loud splash. Someone on the

THE END OF CALICO JACK

sloop, the captain probably, had been fed to the sharks. Then things quieted down and the sloop's cargo was hauled aboard the *William*. Its crew marched to the brig, and my wet, stinking livestock-stall cell became even more crowded. As with the *Nuestra Señora de Riqueza*, the sloop was set ablaze and we sailed away.

Another day, another prize. Calico Jack's appetite for treasure seemed to have no end.

For more than a week we conducted a series of raids along the coast of the western end of Jamaica. Calico Jack's men captured a schooner, sloop, and then, as night approached off Negril Point, a turtle fisherman. This proved to be a fatal mistake. While anchored just off shore in Bry Harbour Bay, the men aboard the turtle fisherman, whether out of fear or a desire to become pirates themselves, treated Calico Jack and his crew to a bowl of rum punch.

As dusk turned to night there came laughing and singing and the occasional shot fired into the air. First one man and then another claimed he'd shot a star from the sky. Soon the party devolved into a drunken brawl, as such festivities almost always did with Calico Jack's crew. Then came a cry of "Sail ho!" (Fancy pirate sailing term that usually means: "Look! There be a huge ship! Let's try to capture it!" but in this case it meant: "Yikes! There be a huge British warship! Let's get out of here!")

Anne Bonny appeared in the brig moments later, freed all prisoners, and issued us pistols and cutlasses.

"What're we doing?" I asked.

"Fighting."

"Fighting?" I repeated unnecessarily.

"Or die trying." Something in her eyes, in her expression, told me she was scared. I knew she'd never admit to being scared: that was not her way. But I could tell she was worried. "Rest of the crew is too drunk to wage a defense. It is you, me, Mary, and these men."

As you can imagine I did not have a good feeling about our chances.

Freed from our livestock-stall cells, me and the rest of the prisoners rushed up the ladder and onto the deck. If the poor souls with me thought this was their chance to escape, they were mistaken. British sailors fanned out, encircling us. Not one of Calico Jack's crew remained on deck; they'd all jumped ship or were cowering below. When the prisoners saw the hopelessness of the situation they dropped to their knees and with hands clasped, begged for mercy.

All but me. I raised my cutlass. Even now I don't know why. Some days I'm just stupid that way.

From within the thick clot of British sailors came an all-too-familiar voice. "I'll gut you like a grouper, you stupid guppy."

I started to ask, "How'd you survive the …?"

"Left me for dead, you did." Jack Sparrow advanced, his sword jabbing and slicing air. "But dead I not be." Scary Mary took a step forward as if to come to my aid, but Jack Sparrow quickly swung his sword in her direction to warn her off. "I got no quarrel with you two ladies. It's the boy I want."

"I have matters to settle with you," Scary Mary said.

Right then two soldiers grabbed and lifted her feet off the deck, and while a third tied her ankles, a fourth soldier bound her wrists. It was clear from the heavy contingent of British sailors and soldiers that Scary Mary would never return to her establishment. Her end was at hand: as was mine if I couldn't think of some way to escape and fast.

I lifted the heavy cutlass and prepared to fight. Jack Sparrow smiled as he thrust and jabbed and did all the things someone trained in fencing might. Me? I backed away while holding the cutlass in front of me. My legs wobbled from fatigue, sweat ran into my eyes. Wrists and arms ached from the weight of the cutlass. (A normal cutlass weighs around four pounds, which may not seem all that heavy, but try swinging four pounds for a few seconds and see how quickly you tire.)

"Should not have run from that tree house." Jack Sparrow said this without the slightest hint of fatigue.

"You were trying to kill me."

Jack Sparrow was incredibly agile for someone who looked like a fictional character and the main protagonist of the "Pirates of the Caribbean" film series. He came at me, bouncing on the balls of his feet, and jabbed at my midsection. I fell for his feinting move, sucking in my gut while bending forward, and nearly lost my head when the tip of his blade nicked my Adam's apple.

"You're quick, guppy. I'll give you that. Excellent form. But how's your footwork?"

He jabbed; I crabbed. He stabbed; I backed away toward the rail behind me.

"If I step here …" Jack Sparrow cross-stepped to his right. I mirrored his move. "Very good. Now I step again."

I gave him a hard stutter-step to my right and broke left. It is the sort of move any decent point guard might make against a larger, slower opponent.

And it almost worked.

His sword whooshed past my ear and struck the railing with a resounding thud. Momentum carried him forward and he slammed his shoulder into my chest, causing me to drop the cutlass.

Stepping back, he lifted his sword to finish me, then hesitated. "Pick it up."

The two of us faced each other, our breathing hard and fast.

Muscles burned, fingers and palm felt greasy-slick with blood from where he'd nicked my elbow. I eyed the cutlass at my feet. "You'll kill me."

"Pick it up."

"No."

He arched an eyebrow. "Come on, guppy, make a show of it. Stop acting like a sissy girl."

Calling me *sissy girl* roused me. I dove at his feet before he could react, smashing into his left ankle and buckling it. I felt the joint snap, heard the crunch of ligaments tearing. Hopping on one foot and screaming in pain, he shifted the sword to his other hand, I suppose to give him better balance on his good ankle.

His hesitation was the opening I needed.

I surprised him with two quick shots to the mouth, then an uppercut to his chin. He winced and gave me a bloody grin. Tossing aside his sword, he came prowling toward me, moving the way a heavyweight boxer does when he's winding up for a knockout punch. This was not the Jack Sparrow of the movies. He was muscular in ways Johnny Depp is not and wanted me dead.

I faked left, but he'd seen that move already. He pummeled me on my cheeks, the side of my head, sides of my arms, mouth, eye … I dropped to my knees, rolled and rolled and rolled and came up with the cutlass.

Swinging the blade wildly at footsteps behind me, it connected with ankle bone.

He went down in a shrill, boyish cry, both hands grabbing his bad ankle.

I bounded up and stood over him, noting the mixture of terror and pain on his face, and pressed the curved edge of the cutlass' blade against his throat.

"Please do not," Anne Bonny called. "They will make you suffer horribly if you do."

It was my moment of glory, a solitary victory among a crew of cowards. But there would be no end to the fighting and cutting until the soldiers rushed and killed me.

I dropped the cutlass.

CHAPTER THIRTY FOUR

THE END OF CALICO JACK

Calico Jack, Anne Bonny, and Scary Mary Read were brought to Spanish Town, Jamaica, along with the rest of us. As word leaked that women pirates were part of our crew, their trials became a big sensation.

On November 16, Calico Jack, Grinning George Fetherston (Master), Richard Corner Pocket (Quartermaster), Little John Davis, and Little John Howell were tried in Port Royal and convicted of piracy. All were sentenced to hang at Gallows Point.

Anne Bonny visited Calico Jack one last time before his execution. Rather than consoling him and calling him "love," as she was fond of doing, she accused Calico Jack of behaving as a coward while she and Scary Mary sought to rally the prisoners and crew for a fight. "Had you fought like a man, you need not have been hanged like a dog."

On November 17, crew members John "Old Dad the Cooper"—or as our crew called him, Fearless Fenis Fenwick—

THE END OF CALICO JACK

and Thomas Bourn (alias Brown) were separately tried and convicted for mutinies committed in mid-June 1720 off Hispaniola.

The next day Calico Jack was hanged gibbet-style and put on display on a small islet called Deadman's Cay near the harbor entrance of Port Royal.

Hobbling James Dobbin, Patrick "Patty Cake" Carty, Thomas Earl, and Noah Harwood were executed a few days later in Kingston. I felt especially bad for Hobbling James Dobbin, but I suspect he'd known the risks when he'd agreed to sail with pirates.

I learned of all this while "under house arrest" in Barracks Yard. Captain Barnett did not think it safe for me to remain with the rest of the crew for fear one of them might stab me in the back. At least that's what Jack Sparrow told me when he shoved me into a four-by-four wooden hut stationed in the middle of the yard.

"How's it that they put you in charge of me?" I asked.

"Bounty hunter. Tireless. Hardy. Smart. Plus, I got the papers on you. You be mine, guppy."

Except for the *smart* part I couldn't argue.

The hut had no windows: ventilation came by way of a breeze that sometimes blew hard enough to work its way between the slats. Mostly I sat in darkness with my knees pressed to my chin. Obviously, I couldn't stretch out or stand. It was unbelievably hot inside.

Jack Sparrow asked, "Where be the treasure from the *Nuestra Señora de Riqueza?*"

I had no intention of telling him or Captain Barnett about the cave on Coffin Cay. In my mind I still held out hope that I'd get back there some day and find some of it. "The what from who?"

"Change your mind you will," growled Jack Sparrow.

Each day Jack Sparrow would bring me a saucer of stale bread, a cup of water, and a bucket in which I did my business. The bucket remained in the hut until he returned, so the aroma inside the hut was not what you would call pine-scented fresh.

One morning Jack Sparrow announced, "Nine of the men caught drinking with Rackham's crew the night of your capture were tried and convicted."

"Names?"

"Little Elton John Eaton, Edward Bilge Swill Warner, Thomas Baker, Thomas B. Quick, John Cole, Benjamin Palmer, Walter Rouse, John Hanson, and John Howard."

I looked up at Jack Sparrow, squinting against the harsh glare of the morning sun. Him opening the door each morning was the highlight of my day, that's how bad my situation had become.

Except for Edward Bilge Swill Warner, the fate of the men meant nothing to me. "They found Edward Bilge Swill Warner guilty?"

"Tried him in amnesia. That means he wasn't there. Probably fell overboard and drowned while drunk."

Of course Edward Bilge Swill Warner had not fallen over and drowned. His body was in the cave with the treasure on Coffin Cay. And Jack Sparrow probably meant to say absentia, but I wasn't about to correct him.

"Ready to tell us where the treasure is?"

"Distributed. Spent. Gone." I had repeated this numerous times to Jack Sparrow. To Captain Barnett, too. I thought it best in my situation to lie like a pirate. I'm not saying lying was a great plan. Or even a good plan. Which meant I needed a new plan.

Jack Sparrow spat in my face. Then he left.

Later that evening he returned, which was odd, since he never visited at night. When he returned he brought an additional slice of bread and a second cup of water.

THE END OF CALICO JACK

"Anne Bonny and Mary Read were found guilty and sent back to prison." He said this with an air of smugness, as if pleased with this news. Which I suppose he was. Whatever money he owed to Scary Mary Read would no longer have to be paid.

"Not hanged?"

"Both 'pleaded their bellies,' and asked for mercy."

With Anne Bonny's child, I assumed Calico Jack was the father, but with Scary Mary, it was anybody's guess. She was quite popular with the men, which may have been one reason she was briefly voted captain.

"In accordance with English common law, they are allowed to receive a temporary stay of execution until they give birth." Reaching down, he yanked me out by the wrist. "Captain wishes to have a word with you."

My legs were so stiff I could barely walk. Fortunately for me Jack Sparrow couldn't walk too fast either, on account of his ankle being wrapped where I'd whacked it with the cutlass.

Captain Jonathan Barnett met us on the docks under a crescent moon. "Tell me about the treasure taken from the *Nuestra Señora de Riqueza*."

So we were back to that, again. I swallowed several times, trying to work up enough saliva. Finally I said in a hoarse whisper, "It's gone."

"Yes, yes, so you continue to say." He paused to light his pipe.

The rich smell of tobacco smoke mixed with the odors of the ship and waterfront. The night air, though not cold, remained damp from the passing of a recent rain shower. Dehydrated, famished, and weak, I stood before him, shivering. I was slowly dying of disease and starvation.

"Those in your crew who were convicted and sentenced to hang told a different story, of sorts. They said the haul was distributed as is the practice with pirates, but the captain kept a share for himself." Captain Barnett puffed, his gaze fixed upward on the crescent moon. "Lead me to it."

"No idea what you're talking about."

Captain Barnett expelled a cloud of smoke. "Return him to the hut. Reduce his rations by half."

At the news that the abuse and torture would continue, I collapsed. Jack Sparrow began kicking me with his boot, ordering me onto my feet. I lifted my hand, trying to wave him off. Did no good. His kicking continued. The toe of his boot caved in a rib; its heel sheered off a flap of skin on my ear. He stomped my hand, then kicked me in the side again.

"Stop," I wheezed. "Please." Tears streamed down my face.

"Take us to the treasure?"

I nodded.

"Warned you would change your mind, guppy." For good measure he grabbed me by the hair and bounced my chin onto the dock.

Jack Sparrow's vow had proved right; they had broken me.

CHAPTER THIRTY FIVE

Treasure Hunt

At once Captain Barnett ordered his crew to make ready to sail. By late afternoon on the second day, we reached Coffin Cay.

In case you're wondering, I didn't have a great plan for finding the treasure. I wasn't about to take them to the cave. I wasn't about to give Jack Sparrow that sort of satisfaction. But I had to lead Barnett and his men somewhere, so I decided to take them to the creek where I had heard gunshots the night of the beach barbecue. My hope was that some of the men had buried their treasure in that area.

I found the creek without any trouble and led the crew inland. Right away, heavy, boggy ground and matted vegetation slowed our progress. But I could see no sign of digging, no freshly gouged mounds of dirt—which did not encourage me. Continuing inland the woods gradually changed from palms and banana trees to pines. Little by little the base of a low ridge began to steepen ahead. Pine needles covered sandy soil.

Flowering shrubs grew in the broad shadow of the pines. The air was fresh with the scent of evergreens.

We had been walking maybe a half hour when we reached a pretty big evergreen. Beneath its branches a bedding of pine needles looked as though they'd been swept away. Poking up through the dirt were shreds of clothing, flakes of rotting skin, and bones. At once Captain Barnett ordered his men to dig. Before long they'd exposed a rotting corpse. The sight of the victim's remains made the hair on my neck bristle.

The sound of distant breakers crashing on the reef and the whine of countless mosquitoes interrupted the solemn silence. We all stood in a circle looking down at the dead man.

"There," I said, pointing at the pock-marked cliff rising above the forest. "See those three tall boulders?" I pointed up at some rocks near the base of the Skull. "Calico Jack's men stood on those boulders to sight the *William*. That's how they knew where to come back to find where they dug."

I was making all this up. Not a man on the *William* had said anything about "three tall boulders" and I was the only one who called the cliff the "Skull."

"Dig that man out and you'll find treasure, I bet."

Right away the soldiers began digging, taking care to place the man's remains next to the shallow pit. Sure enough, once they'd removed the dead man, the soldiers found two amber glasses filled with jewels and a small leather pouch stuffed with coins. So the rumor was true: pirates would sometimes shoot another crew member and bury treasure under him. I'd read about it in one of my pirate books but never actually found any evidence to support the claim.

The soldiers dug deep and wide, looking for more, but only found the two bottles and one pouch.

"There must be more," Captain Barnett said.

"Oh, sure," I replied. "Lots. But it's scattered all over the island. It'll take days or weeks to find it all."

"Then you had better be about the business of finding it."

"What he said," said Jack Sparrow. "Else, as they say, it'll be two birds felled with one shot."

In case you're wondering, I was not encouraged by the captain's comment. It was clear that at some point soon he would grow tired of the charade, and I'd be a dead man.

I led them into a thicket choked with briars and some plants with razor-sharp fronds. The soldiers wore long pants, shirts, and a few of them still had on coats. Me? I was barefoot and still wore my cargo shorts and a tee. Mostly it was me who got cut by the fronds.

After a few moments of hacking and slashing with swords, we emerged in a small clearing. Before us was a great excavation, not very recent. Its sandy sides had caved in and a few pine cones lay on the bottom. Like the grave we had just uncovered, there were bits of broken boards, shells, and several glass bottles strewn around. Thing was—and this is why I suddenly felt sick to my stomach—the pit was empty. Someone had dug it up. Question was, who?

"What happened to the treasure?" asked Captain Barnett.

"Maybe the dead man we found back there hid in the woods, here, and watched while his fellow shipmate buried treasure. Then when the shipmate headed back to the *William*, the thief dug it up, and took it as his own. Right then another of the crew shot him and took it all for himself."

I admit it was a complicated tale and not likely to impress Captain Barnett, but I had to say something. So the something I said was, "There's more. Lots."

"You keep saying that, but so far it's just two small bottles and a pouch. I know for a fact that the *Nuestra Señora de Riqueza* carried much more than that."

I didn't respond. It seemed like the smart move.

We proceeded up the slope toward the three boulders and then down the backside of the small ridge. Our route took us

THE END OF CALICO JACK

into dense woods. Basically, I was lost. But of course I didn't tell them this. And I tried not to let them know how lost I was.

But I think Jack Sparrow knew.

"Two birds felled with one shot," said Jack Sparrow.

I did not like Jack here or there. I did not like Jack Sparrow anywhere. I did not like him in the jungle or on a ship. I did not like him making me say uncle or at my hip. I did not like Jack Sparrow in my nightmare. I did not like Jack Sparrow anywhere.

Out of the middle of the great stillness, came a beastly breathing noise: a great snorting intake, followed by a long exhalation.

Sniff . . . sigh. Sniff . . . sigh. Sniff . . . sigh.

It was as though a winded dragon lay fallen in the woods.

The soldiers' talking turned to whispering, then stopped all together.

I tried to identify the sound. I hoped it was not a large animal. An animal springing out of the bush and attacking me would definitely not be good. The thought of huge carnivorous animals being on the island had never occurred to me. Far as I knew, the Caribbean islands didn't have lions and tigers and bears or wolves, jaguars, and black panthers. But then, I was back in pirate time, so maybe it was possible there were wild beasts roaming about.

Sniff . . . sigh. Sniff . . . sigh. Sniff . . . sigh.

The sound seemed somehow familiar.

Sniff . . . clank.

Immediately I recognized the sound—and it chilled my heart.

Without a word Captain Barnett raised his sword, signaling to his men, and we charged through the thicket and attacked.

CHAPTER THIRTY SIX

A DEAD MAN'S CHEST

Edward Bilge Swill Warner held a short spade half the length of a baseball bat, but as soon as he saw the soldiers, he backpedaled, dropped the spade, and tumbled backward into the excavated pit.

As with the first crater we had found, small amber bottles lay about on sand and dirt, but there were more of them. Leather pouches, some still bulging with their contents, lay strewn about. On the rim of the pit sat a small wooden box not much larger than Mom's jewelry box. Inside were all manner of rubies, emeralds, and gold coins. Large silver nuggets shimmered in sunlight streaming through the jungle forest. Bilge Swill had been a very busy man—especially for someone so dead.

Captain Barnett ordered the dead man out of the pit. Bilge Swill did so without hesitation. This was partially due to the fact that really, he had no choice. Soldiers aimed muskets at him. Just the same, Jack Sparrow leaned over the rim and poked and prodded him with such force that the poor man jumped each time the tip of Jack Sparrow's bayonet found flesh. I couldn't help but feel sorry for Bilge Swill. Partially because I knew what lay ahead for him, but mostly because once Barnett and his men were finished with Calico Jack's last crew member, Barnett would turn his attention to me.

You may be wondering how Bilge Swill survived getting shot by Calico Jack. And how he'd escaped the cave. I wondered that myself. Of course I didn't ask. We both knew the bulk of the treasure lay in the cave.

"State your name, man."

"Edward Warner, sir. I serve aboard the *William*, a British schooner that sails out of New Providence."

As he said this Bilge Swill locked eyes with me. His meaning seemed clear: *Keep quiet about the cave.*

"You are a pirate," Captain Barnett said.

"No, sir. I'm but a poor seaman who's been put ashore to die."

"Pirate," Captain Barnett restated. "One who's been tried, found guilty, and sentenced to hang at Gallows Point. Which, as soon as we return to Spanish Town, you will surely do."

"I swear on me mum's grave, I never once served before the mast of a pirate ship." Looking about he seemed to size up his situation. I gathered from his expression he did not like his prospects. "Please, sir, me throat is parched. Might I have a sip of water?"

"You will get rations enough once you are in the brig. Fed and bedded and then hanged, those are the accommodations that await you." Captain Barnett gestured at the small box of treasure at the pirate's feet. "How much?"

The poor man's face scrunched up with confusion. "How much what, sir?"

"Treasure from the *Nuestra Señora de Riqueza.*"

"I swear, I was only digging to find a fresh spring. Swamp water gave me the trots."

"The rest of your friends are dead. Hanged for their crimes. So there is no point in continuing this preposterous lie. Where is the rest of the treasure?"

"I swear, sir, I never stole any—"

Before he could finish Jack Sparrow jabbed his bayonet hard in the man's ribs. I think he only meant to prompt the pirate to tell the truth, but at the last moment Bilge Swill shifted his weight, which caused the bayonet to pierce his shirt and flesh. A wound opened and began spewing blood.

Bilge Swill's eyes went wide; his face twisted in pain. He grasped his side with both hands and dropped to his knees. This all happened in, like, two seconds. Happened so fast that it took a moment for Captain Barnett to realize that the one person who possibly knew the location of the *Nuestra Señora de Riqueza* treasure lay bleeding to death.

"Fool!" Captain Barnett snatched the bayonet-musket from Jack Sparrow. "Quick, men! Help him!"

Two soldiers rushed forward and applied pressure on the wound. When that didn't slow the bleeding, they rolled Bilge Swill onto his back and, ripping his shirt apart, tried to stuff strips into the crimson cavity. Slowly his face turned from sunburnished bronze to pale gray. The dying man's eyes remained fixed on the jungle foliage overhead, but no longer did he look left or right, only straight up. Blinking every few seconds, he took short, shallow breaths.

Captain Barnett rushed to his side and knelt. "Tell me man, where is the rest? Where is the treasure?" Barnett pressed his ear to the pirate's lips.

Edward Warner's mouth sagged. He swallowed once and, rolling his head, fixed his eyes on me. A ghastly, rattling exhalation escaped his lips. It was his last. The dead pirate was indeed dead.

"Fool!" Captain Barnett repeated. "String him up."

THE END OF CALICO JACK

I admit: hearing that Jack Sparrow would hang for his bumbling mistake made me smile. But my smile quickly faded when a noose was hurriedly fashioned and shoved over my head.

"Wait! How's this my fault?"

"Put him on that idiot bounty hunter's shoulders."

Jack Sparrow appeared none too pleased with this news. His ankle was still wrapped from where I'd whacked it with the cutlass. I'm sure walking in swamps and on sandy soil had not helped. Two of Captain Barnett's men shoved Jack Sparrow to his knees, swung my legs over his shoulders, and yanked Sparrow up by his elbows.

Struggling under my weight, Jack Sparrow straightened to his full height.

Another soldier threw the other end of the rope over a stout tree branch and pulled it tight.

"Ricky Bradshaw, inasmuch as you have been tried and convicted of the high crime of piracy, plus some other infractions that we do not have time to recount, I sentence you to death by hanging. Is there anything you wish to say?"

I tried to protest, but the rope was too tight.

"Very well. Shoot him."

The command stunned me. I'd thought Captain Barnett meant to hang me. But now it seemed I would face a firing squad. A soldier raised his rifle, aimed, and … shot Jack Sparrow.

He fell.

I fell.

Two birds felled with one shot.

170

CHAPTER THIRTY SEVEN

A Tale Worth Its Weight In Gold

"Ricky . . . you with me?"
"Ricky?"
"Ricky . . . blink if you hear me?"

I squint against the harshness of the sun and swallow.

Mom shakes me by the shoulder. "You okay?

I look right at Mom but don't really see her. It's the feeling you have when you're daydreaming and look straight at someone but aren't really focused on the person.

"You're scratching. Stop scratching." Mom gently pulls my hands away from my throat.

Only now do I realize that I'm clawing and tugging as if to pull away a noose.

Mom puts both her hands on the sides of my head. "Look at me."

My fixed stare melts and slowly I begin to take in my surroundings: Mom, Dad, the front of the motorboat. The blue water all around and the island ahead with green mountains rising towards clouds.

"I'm okay," I say.

Dad studies me with a look of concern. I realized this is the first time he has seen me experience an episode. "You sure you're okay?"

I rub my throat, check my sides where Jack Sparrow pounded his fists into me, then my jaw and teeth. "Think so, yeah."

Dad cuts his gaze towards Mom. She looks away, thumbs a tear.

I glance around. "Your handbag?"

"We hit a big wave." Dad gestures back to the driver. "We tried, honest we did. He wheeled this boat around but your mom's handbag was already gone."

So no ship's log, I think. *No ledger with the* Nuestra Señora de Riqueza's *treasure listed. Nothing to show for our trip to Coffin Cay.*

Mom folds my hands in my lap. I make no attempt to resist. I'm still not 100 percent focusing. It's like that feeling you have when you're waking up from a hard sleep. Reality and dreams mix.

Her fingers bump against something hard beneath damp fabric. "What's that?"

I slide my hand into a pocket. I stare at the object. "A key."

"I can see that. Where did you get it?"

It's the skeleton key. Other than being wet with sea spray it's exactly as Calico Jack gave it to me.

"What's it do?" Dad asks.

I pivot on the bench seat and look at the driver standing at the console—then past at the ominous dark clouds gathering over Coffin Cay. Lightning explodes, creating a momentary burst of orange where the sun should be. Then the veil of darkness swallows the light as the rumble of thunder reaches us. "We have to go back."

"You wish to go back?" the skipper asks.

"No, we're not going back," Mom says.

Still looking off towards the small bump that's Coffin Cay, I say, "Mom, we have to. It's back there."

"What's back there?" asks Dad.

"Take us back to the marina," Mom says. "And it looks like you better hurry."

"The treasure," I say to Dad. "Please?"

Out of the corner of my eye I see Mom shaking her head.

Dad places his hand on my shoulder, leans close, and locks eyes with me as if trying to figure out if I'm really in my right mind. "You sure?"

"Frank, you can't possibly be serious?"

"It's there, Dad. Not all of it. Only a little. Some coins and emeralds and rubies. But it's a real treasure and I know right where to look."

The thunder booms closer. The band of blackness uses up more of the sky.

"Turn the boat around," Dad says to the skipper. "We're going back."

But, of course, we do not. At that moment the first big drops fall, splatting almost unnoticed on my bare knees. Our hunt for the treasure is over.

But my story is not.

Because you know where the treasure is. I have provided you with a map and told you things that only someone who was there will know. If you think I'm lying, check it out for yourself. Coffin Cay is still off the western tip of Haiti. You can learn some things about Calico Jack online but it's best to buy books and dig into the archival documents found at museums, mostly in Great Britain. Do all this and you will find my story checks out.

But if not, if someone else gets to the treasure first, remember this: it's not the destination that brings joy, but the journey.

THE END OF CALICO JACK

And the people you meet.
And the places you go.
And the way the intense heat and pressure that come from tough times shape you into something better than what you were before.
Something rare.
Something precious.
Something worth its weight in gold.
~ Ricky Bradshaw

The Routes of Calico Jack

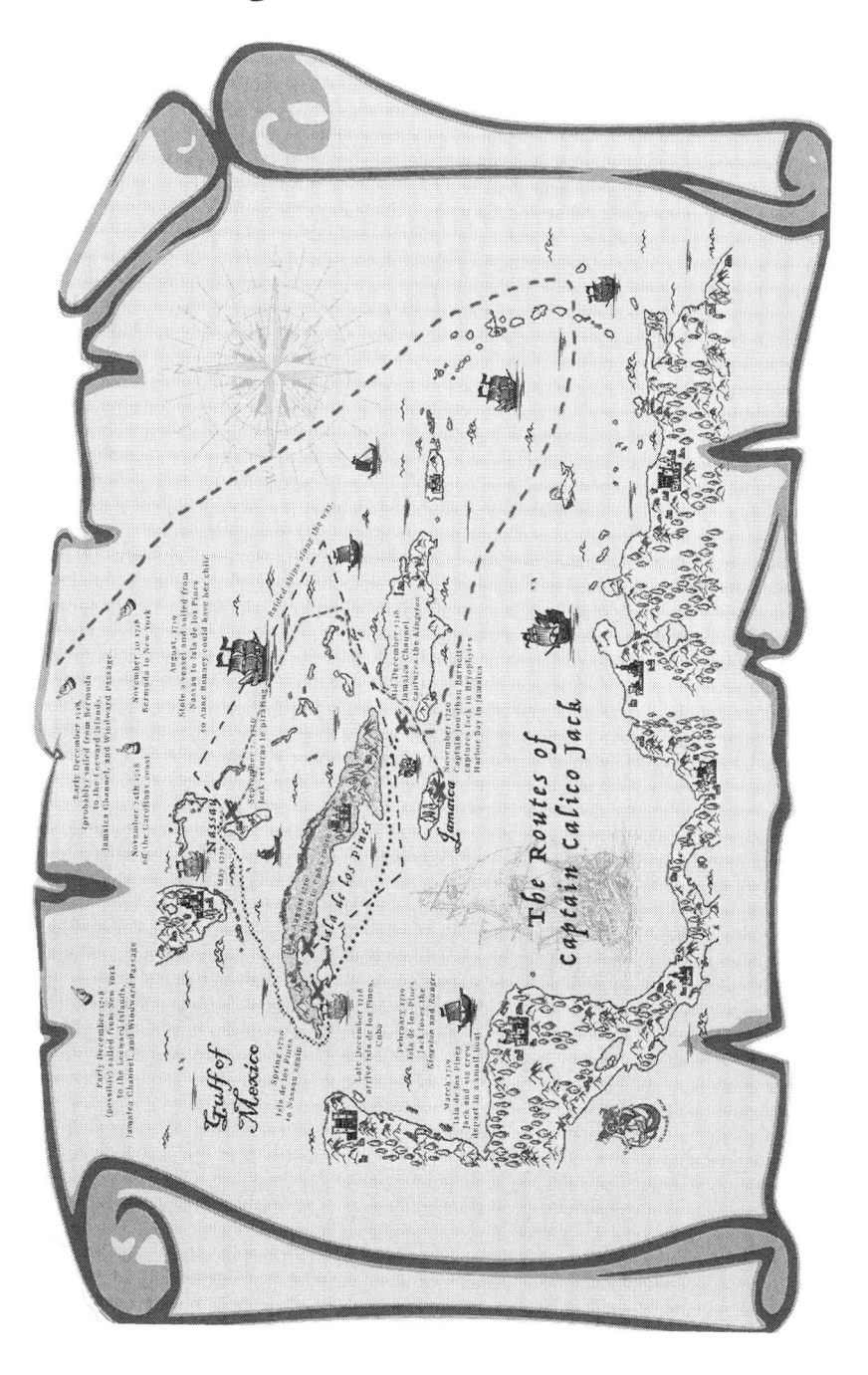

AN HISTORICAL ACCOUNT OF CALICO JACK

Calico Jack, a.k.a. John Rackham, was born in December 1682. His nickname is derived from the calico clothing he wore. Jack is a nickname for "John." What follows is a close approximation of his sailing adventures during his brief pirate career.

July 1718, Nassau

On July 22, 1718, Woodes Rogers arrived in Nassau to address the problem of piracy in the Caribbean. There he surprised and trapped a ship commanded by pirate Charles Vane. No doubt John Rackham, serving as quartermaster, was aboard with Vane at the time. Woodes offered Vane and his men a chance to surrender. Vane responded by using a captured French vessel as a fireship in an attempt to ram the naval blockade. The attempt failed, but the British warships were forced out of the west end of Nassau harbor, giving Vane's crew an opportunity to raid the town and secure the best local pilot. Vane and his men then escaped in a small sloop (probably the *Neptune* or *Treasure*) via the harbor's narrow east entrance. The pirates had evaded the trap, but Nassau and New Providence Island were firmly in Rogers' hands.

November 24, 1718, off the Carolinas coast

In November 1718, Jack Rackham served as quartermaster on a British sloop, the *Neptune* or *Treasure,* sailing under Captain Charles Vane. Vane and his crew raided ships off the United States eastern seaboard, targeting smaller fishing boats and

THE END OF CALICO JACK

other vessels unlikely to put up a fight. In mid-November, a French warship was spotted. The ship was at least twice as large as the *Neptune*. Vane gave the order to leave the area. Most of the crew argued that the French vessel would make a fine prize and surely have more loot than the smaller ships they had been taking. The bigger the ship, the bigger the haul for all. The decision to attack was put to a vote; Vane lost 75 to 15. Despite overwhelming support for Jack Rackham and his demand that they stay and fight, Vane ordered the *Neptune* to flee. On November 24, 1718, charging Vane with cowardice, the crew voted him out and made Jack Rackham captain of the *Neptune*.

November 30, 1718, Bermuda to New York

Some accounts claim the crew marooned Vane, along with fifteen other crew members, on a small island off Bermuda. Other accounts argue that the crew set Vane and his fifteen supporters adrift in a smaller boat, along with a small supply of ammunition and goods. Some historians claim Jack and his crew then sailed for New York. More likely, Jack put Vane and the fifteen ashore off Bermuda and sailed south where he set about plundering ships around the Leeward Islands.

Early December 1718, Jamaica Channel

Sometime in early December, Jack and his men reached the West Indies but found only smaller ships. Having sailed down the Windward and Leeward Islands, the *Neptune*, (now renamed the *Ranger*,) turned west then northwest, and sailed towards Hispaniola, Jamaica, and Cuba. There, in Jamaica Channel, Jack came upon his first big prize: an English merchant ship called the *Kingston*. The *Ranger* quickly captured the *Kingston*, a large prize. The ship had a rich cargo, and the ecstatic crew made the *Kingston* their new flagship. Unfortunately, the *Kingston* was taken within sight of Port Royal. Local merchants, upset by the taking of *their* goods, outfitted pirate-hunting Spanish ships in order to capture and punish Jack and his men.

Late December of 1718, Isla de los Pines, Cuba

Historians dispute the timing of the events that followed, but evidently Jack and his men managed to avoid the pirate-hunters and sailed for Isla de los Pines (Isla de la Juventud), Cuba. The hunting party surprised Jack and his men in February 1719 as most of his crew dozed ashore in a camp of tents made from old sails. With the *Kingston* and *Ranger* lightly guarded, the bounty hunter's crew simply boarded the two vessels, overpowered the skeleton crew, and sailed away while Jack and his men hid in the woods.

March or April 1719, Isla de los Pines

Some weeks after Jack lost his fleet, he and six other crew members left Isla de los Pines in a small boat. For the next few days, they sailed towards Nassau, probably by way of the Straits of Florida. With Cuba to the south, they rode the Gulf Stream north before turning east towards Nassau.

May 1719, Nassau

When Jack and his six men arrived in May 1719, the island's population consisted of about two hundred former pirates and several hundred fugitives who had escaped from nearby Spanish colonies. In a years time Rogers had organized a government. To those former pirates on the island who had not yet surrendered,

THE END OF CALICO JACK

he once more offered the King's Pardon. Rogers' proposal was simple enough: any pirate would be pardoned in exchange for discontinuing their illegal endeavors.

There, while frequenting the taverns, Jack met Anne Bonny. Though she was married to James Bonny (or John Bonny)—a petty pirate who now made a meager living informing Rogers of the activities and whereabouts of his former mates—Anne and Jack began to have an affair. When James Bonny found out about the relationship, Jack offered to buy Anne in a "divorce by purchase." James Bonny refused. Faced with this setback, Jack and his crew asked for the pardon, claiming that Vane had forced them to become pirates. Rogers, who hated Vane, due in part to the way Vane had escaped the previous summer, granted them a pardon with the stipulation that they would be put to death if they ever again returned to piracy. Jack, still involved with Anne, moved onto New Providence and settled into the life of a *reformed* pirate.

When Anne became pregnant with Jack's child, James Bonny husband attempted to have Anne convicted of adultery and whipped. Clearly, the peaceful retirement from piracy Jack sought was proving difficult. Rather than leave Anne behind to be flogged, the pair began assembling a crew. In August of 1719, Jack, Anne Bonny, Mary Read, and a handful of other disgruntled ex-pirates stole a sloop late at night and slipped out of Nassau's harbor.

Jack's decision to allow Anne to sail with him was unusual; women were considered bad luck aboard ships. Fearing that the crew would refuse to sail alongside a woman, Anne dressed as a man and sailed under the name Adam Bonny. (Other historians claim that Mary Read joined the crew when she met Jack and Anne in Cuba.)

August 1719, Nassau to Cuba (Isla de los Pines)

For the remainder of the year, the new crew attacked fishermen and poorly armed merchants, mostly in the waters off of Jamaica. The crew swiftly earned a reputation for ruthlessness, particularly the two women, who dressed like, fought, and swore just as their male companions. Dorothy Thomas, a fisherwoman whose boat was captured by Jack's crew, testified that Bonny and Read had demanded the crew murder Thomas so that she could not testify against them. Thomas further swore that if it were not for their large breasts, she would not have known that Bonny and Read were women.

For several months they sailed the Caribbean. In addition to targeting merchant traders and fishermen, Jack also attacked smaller pirate vessels, often inviting—or forcing—captured crew members to serve with him. With an ever-expanding force of pirates under his command, Jack managed to cause chaos in the Caribbean.

Ann Bonny's fellow shipmates soon grew suspicious of her gender. She ceased the ruse, though when participating in armed conflict and pillaging stolen vessels, she continued to disguise herself as a man. In late 1719 or early 1720, Jack's crew reached Cuba. There Anne gave birth to her first child.

Spring 1720, Isla de los Pines

After the birth of their child in the early spring of 1720, while Jack and his crew were refitting their vessel, a Spanish warship towing a captured English sloop spied Jack's vessel anchored in a cove on Isla de los Pines. Though Jack and his crew were aboard and trapped, the warship could not reach them due

THE END OF CALICO JACK

to low tide. The captain of the warship decided to anchor in the harbor entrance to wait for morning. That night, perhaps recalling how Vane had escaped Rogers' trap in the summer of 1718, Jack, the two women, and his crew rowed over to the captured English sloop. They overpowered the Spanish sailors guarding the vessel and took command. As dawn broke, the warship began blasting Jack's old ship, now empty. With Jack's child left in the care of some pirate families in Cuba, he and his crew silently sailed past the Spanish warship in their new vessel. What became of Jack's child is unknown.

August 1720, Nassau

Jack, Anne, Mary, and ten others (or more) arrived in Nassau in August. On August 22, while strolling the docks of Nassau, the crew climbed aboard a 12-ton sloop called the *William*, owned by John Ham, and sailed away. It would be the last time Jack sailed from New Providence.

September 2, 1720, Nassau

Though the warrant for Jack's capture was not published until October 1720, in September Woodes Rogers issued a proclamation declaring Jack and his crew pirates. After publication of the warrant, pirate hunter Captain Jonathan Barnet and former pirate Jean Bonadvis went in search of the *William*.

Within three months of returning to piracy, the crew of the *William* (renamed the *Revenge*) had plundered the equivalent of $1.5 million U.S. dollars from merchant traders and fishing vessels. (This amount is more likely the *sum total* of Jack's take during his career, not his final three months.) It seems Jack and his crew spent most of those three months south of the Bahamas in the area of Jamaica, Cuba, and Hispaniola where they captured numerous small fishing vessels and terrorized fishermen along the northern Jamaican coastline.

October 1720, Jamaica

In late October or early November, the *Ranger* encountered a small vessel crewed by nine English pirates. The nine joined Jack on his ship for a bout of drinking while at anchor in Bry Harbour Bay. As night wore on and a deep fog moved in, one of Jack's crew fired his gun at a bird. As fate would have it, Captain Jonathan Barnet's vessel lay within earshot. Unable to spot the ship in the dark and fog, Barnet called out for the vessel to identify itself, to which Jack replied "Jack Rackham, New Providence." Barnet had found his man. Had Jack not been so drunk, he may not have fallen for the trick. Barnet ordered his guns to fire on the spot where the sound had originated. His ship let loose with all guns. The *Revenge* was hit with a full broadside, destroying its rudder and setting it adrift. Barnet's men boarded the *Revenge*. After a brief but fierce fight presumably led by Mary Read and Anne Bonny, Barnet's men captured the *William*. Jack's reign of terror was over.

November 1720, Jamaica

Jack and his crew were brought to trial at St. Jago De La Vega (Spanish Town) in Jamaica on November 16, 1720. It is reputed that Jack tried to strike a deal with the governor under which he would surrender himself if clemency were given to Anne and Mary Read. Whether or not this is true, the two women escaped the noose by claiming to be pregnant. Jack was tried, convicted of piracy, and sentenced to hang. On November

THE END OF CALICO JACK

18, 1720 in Port Royal, he was executed along with George Fetherston (Master), Richard Corner (Quartermaster), and John Davis. As a warning to would-be pirates, Jack's body was tarred and hanged in a cage (*gibbeted*) at the harbor entrance of Port Royal. The remaining members of Jack's crew were found guilty of piracy. Most were hanged the next day.

Anne Bonny and Mary Read both claimed to be pregnant at their trials. Ten days after Jack's execution, they were given a temporary stay until the claim was proven. Read died in April 1721, most likely of fever related to childbirth. There is no official historical record of Anne Bonny's release, execution, or death. Some say Anne died in prison. Others claim she escaped and reverted to her life as a pirate. According to the Oxford Dictionary of National Biography (2004), Anne Bonny's father paid the ransom for his daughter and brought her back to Charles Town (Charleston) in South Carolina, where in 1721 she married her second husband, Joseph Burleigh. They had eight children. She died on April 25, 1782, in South Carolina.

The day after Jack's trial, former crew members John "Old Dad the Cooper" (or "Fenis" Fenwick) and Thomas Bourn (alias Brown) were separately tried and convicted for mutinies committed in mid-June 1720 off Hispaniola. Patrick Carty, Thomas Earl, James Dobbin, and Noah Harwood were executed in Kingston.

Nine men who had been caught drinking with Rackham's crew (John Eaton, Edward Warner, Thomas Baker, Thomas Quick, John Cole, Benjamin Palmer, Walter Rouse, John Hanson, and John Howard) were tried and convicted on January 24, 1721. On February 17, John Eaton, Thomas Quick, and Thomas Baker were executed at Gallows Point at Port Royal. The next day John Cole, John Howard, and Benjamin Palmer were executed at Kingston. The execution dates of Edward Warner, Walter Rouse, and John Hanson is unknown.

In addition to his preference for calico clothing, Jack Rackham is also known for his version of the Jolly Roger flag with its black background, white human skull, and two crossed swords.

Printed in Great Britain
by Amazon